CONCILI

CONCILIUM
ADVISORY COMMITTEE

CONCILIUM   2010/3

HUMAN NATURE AND NATURAL LAW

Edited by

Lisa Sowle Cahill, Hille Haker, and
Eloi Messi Metogo

SCM Press · London

Published by SCM Press, 13–17 Long Lane, London EC1A 9PN

Copyright © International Association of Conciliar Theology, Madras (India)

www.concilium.in

English translations copyright © 2010 Hymns Ancient and Modern Ltd

ISBN 978 0 334 03109 3

Printed in the UK by
CPI Antony Rowe, Chippenham, Wiltshire

Concilium published March, June, August, October,
December

Contents

Part Two: Theological Forum

Editorial
Human Nature and Natural Law:
A Critical Discussion

The primary traditional basis of Roman Catholic ethics and politics is the 'natural law.' In his 2009 encyclical *Caritas in veritate*, Benedict XVI asserts, 'In all cultures there are examples of ethical convergence, some isolated, some interrelated, as an expression of the one human nature, willed by the Creator; the tradition of ethical wisdom knows this as the natural law. This universal moral law provides a sound basis for all cultural, religious and political dialogue. . . .' (no. 59). Also in 2009, the International Theological Commission issued a document called *The Search for a Universal Ethic: A New Look at Natural Law*. The ITC proposes the natural law as a resource for meeting global ethical challenges. The advantage of natural law is its affirmation that 'persons and the human community are capable, by the light of reason, of knowing the fundamental guidelines for moral action in conformity with the very nature of the human subject, and of expressing them in a normative manner, in the form of precepts or commandments' (no. 9).

These documents attest to the fact that Catholic magisterial teaching, moral theology, and social thought still retain a central place for the basic ideas behind natural law theory. For example, all human beings share a common nature, nature is created by God and can be known by human reason, and the goods that all persons seek by nature are the basis of moral norms that prescribe what kinds of actions do or do not fulfill human goods. The normative value of natural law comes from the fact that it directs human beings to their proper ends and corresponding actions, and it is by fulfilling their natural ends that humans flourish and find happiness.

Types of natural law ethics appear in classic Greek and Latin philosophers, as well as in the Bible. Catholic natural law ethics is given its distinctive flavour and vocabulary by the thirteenth-century theologian Thomas Aquinas. Neo-Scholastic interpretations of Aquinas's theory of the natural law were prevalent in eighteenth- and nineteenth-century Catholicism, but their influence waned following the Second Vatican Council.

Criticisms frequently are brought against natural law's deductive method, Eurocentric and patriarchal biases, abstract universalism, and neglect of distinctive Christian ethics and traditions. Moreover, many argue that nature cannot serve as a norm at all, since an 'ought' cannot be derived from an 'is' (David Hume and G. E. Moore) and since human nature itself is constantly evolving rather than static. The defence of the concept 'human nature' as a basis of clear and stable norms has become even more difficult as a result of new scientific research and discoveries indicating the continuity of human nature with other animals, and offering the possibility to make radical changes in life forms, including human beings.

The end of the twentieth and beginning of the twenty-first centuries reveal an impressive variety of culturally different ethics around the globe, newly visible by modern communications media. Yet the very fact of world-wide conflict, violence, and environmental danger seems to cry out for global ways to define what true 'humanization' means (Jon Sobrino), and to endorse some shared vocabulary like 'human goods' or 'human rights' to advance international cooperation to end poverty, violence, and oppression.

Therefore an array of thinkers, especially from the Catholic tradition, are searching for new ways to retrieve, renegotiate, and reinvent concepts of common human nature, goods, values, and rights. This issue of *Concilium* will display some of this new thinking, in order to explore whether natural law is still a useful ethical and political framework, and whether it can be expanded in light of new cultural, philosophical, and scientific perspectives and challenges. It will also discuss whether disregard of historical reasoning is an inherent part of the natural law tradition, or whether natural law reasoning can be successfully modified using more historical and culturally sensitive approaches.

This issue includes eight major essays on the basic theory of natural law, and four shorter essays. Among the latter, two are discussions of recent documents that bear on natural law concepts: the ITC report mentioned above, and a new document from the European Union on synthetic biology. The other two test natural law by looking at torture and ecology. Our authors do not all adopt the same theological, philosophical, cultural, and scientific resources, nor do they all agree as to the nature and future of natural law ethics. Together, they produce a lively and provocative discussion of the prospects for some level of universality and historical continuity at the level of normative judgments in ethics and politics.

Stephen J. Pope presents the origins of the central and most influential strand of Catholic natural law thinking in the 'moral realism' of Thomas Aquinas. According to Aquinas, natural law is the rational creature's participation in the divine law that reasonably orders the universe for the common good. Practical reason discerns the means to the achievement of human goods. Because humans are social creatures, pursuit of human goods and observance of the natural law are social activities and involve social responsibilities. Though humans have an innate capacity to know the good, the capacity to discern the good correctly and act on it has to be formed so that it is habitual or virtuous. The virtues facilitate judgments, choices, and actions that are in accord with the natural law. Positive law, based on the natural law, determines how the human goods and good community are realized in concrete cultures and circumstances.

Pope discusses two major contemporary challenges to natural law thinking: cultural pluralism and evolutionary theory. Earlier thinkers such as Francisco de Vitoria and Bartolomé de Las Cases adapted natural theory for the international context. In the twentieth century, others such as Jacques Maritain and John Courtney Murray reinterpreted Catholic natural law to support liberal democracy and human rights. A continuing challenge is to make international, universalistic arguments while respecting cultural pluralism. Darwin's theory of evolution also challenges natural law by undermining the idea that nature consists in a fixed hierarchy of species directly created by God. A critical re-appropriation of evolutionary science will allow natural law theorists to achieve a greater appreciation of diversity among humans and other species, and therefore of the complexity of the good or goods.

Andrés Torres Queiruga takes up the theological perspective within which natural law has been viewed in the Christian tradition, including the relation of natural law to revelation. He considers the impact on natural law of modern secularization and epistemology. In different cultural and religious traditions, the idea of 'nature' is a way of expressing that biological and social life are ordered rather than chaotic. However, modernity has broken the supposed derivation of this order from a revealed divine law. It overturns any philosophical or theological idealism holding that being exists in descendent gradations, or that deductive reason can reflect the immutability and universality of eternal realities.

Ethics and morality interpret natural dynamisms, whose ethical meaning must be discovered. The problem is to maintain both the objective foundation of norms, against voluntarism and legal positivism; and at the same time to recognize historical variability. The thought of Angel Amor Ruibal shows that the ethical arises from original, a-thematic, universal, and indefinite experiences, which can be oriented by categories such as 'life' or 'conscience.' These take on different concrete meanings without *a priori* limits. The fundamental ethical absolute is to seek good and avoid evil, but the practical meaning of good and evil must be discovered with the help of human knowledge. The role of the religions in this process is to provide an intentionality and motivation that includes all persons within the love of God. Sometimes this intentionality absolutely excludes specific concrete moral contents, as in the case of infanticide. But many ethical questions are much less clear. Nevertheless, the irreducible intentionality of faith or religion makes a valuable contribution to the common good of humanity.

Eberhard Schockenhoff offers a new, transcendental foundation of Thomas Aquinas' doctrine of natural law, in a re-reading informed by Kant. Thomas' concept of natural law is not to be interpreted as a theory of a-historical truth that leaves no room for individuals' concepts of the good life. Read with a Kantian interpretation, natural law refers to the transcendental conditions of moral agency on the one hand, and 'substantive' conceptions of the good life as constitutive parts of the individual's identity on the other hand.

The transcendental interpretation of natural law articulates certain basic conditions of moral agency, which are the human goods, along with fundamental freedom and autonomy. These conditions are captured by Kant's concept of human dignity. To live in accordance with one's own nature means to strive for the realization of one's capabilities, guided by practical reason. Thus 'to live in accordance with nature' needs the perspective of 'interested participants,' oriented concretely by different worldviews, values, and goals. The transcendental interpretation of natural law does not prescribe a comprehensive concept of the good life. 'Nature' is not a static but a dynamic concept. This, Schockenhoff holds, is reflected in different interpretations of the 'meaning of life', such as the one offered in the Christian tradition.

Ludwig Siep addresses the traces of the natural law tradition in contemporary debates on bioethics. One basic question is whether 'nature' is merely the material and object of humans' will to change, construct, or design biological organisms, leaving no place for an evaluative or normative dimension of 'nature.' A second question is whether there is something 'right according to nature' (*physei dikaion*), a foundation for moral norms that limit democratic or legal decisions.

The concept of nature presupposed in many bioethical debates is more or less the one brought forward by the sciences: object of intervention and change, dependent and explicable in causal and functional terms, with no value 'in itself.' Bio*ethics* is then understood as the process of regulation and justification of norms that are of practical (or pragmatic) relevance. If the tradition of natural law is relevant at all, it is so because it provides an evaluative and normative structure. Siep argues that even though it is problematic to retain the concept of natural law, the *legacy* of this tradition is threefold: it explicates the question of the valuable dimension of natural processes, it brings openness to experiences in the political sphere, and it affirms the individual's freedom of conviction. In his examples Siep shows that it is this legacy that enables us to find reasonable arguments for some of the fundamental bioethical controversies.

Jean-Pierre Wils confronts the natural law tradition with several critical questions including its static character, culture-insensitive universalism, and abstraction from concrete analyses of circumstances. With Michael Walzer, Wils argues that universalism is a two-dimensional concept; it entails the 'thick' faces of moral experiences, but also the 'thin' concepts related to a shared humanity. The experiential-hermeneutical dimension cannot be taken as universally valid, while the normative albeit abstract universalism conceals its own genesis in historical situations. Yet *together* these dimensions are encoded in moral concepts. We do have – and in fact need – points of views that come from 'somewhere,' for we live in contexts that are already structured. The question is not whether we can 'invent' or 'discover' moral claims but whether we find the appropriate interpretation in a given moral situation or conflict.

The legacy of the natural law tradition lies in this dynamic of interpretation and normative claims. 'Situations' are dynamic, but normative claims are also, in that they require contextualized interpretation. Universal norms stem from comparable (not from the same) experiences, and are subject to ongoing reinterpretation in view of new experiences. Reinterpretation of 'natural law' today should embrace this dynamic interpretation and reflective analysis,

Cristina Traina sees revised natural law thinking as an asset to feminist theory and theology. A critical version of natural law can base justice advocacy on enduring moral limits and well as on intellectual humility. Traina reviews Thomas Aquinas' theory of natural law, emphasizing that natural law encourages the human organization of societies and international relations to support the flourishing of all. Natural law places its vision of the good life within a framework of divine providence, holistic flourishing, and the acknowledgment of sin. Traina notes that Aquinas embraced immutable hierarchies of gender, class, vocation, and so on, which runs counter to feminist visions of justice today. Moreover, recent magisterial teaching has tended to dismiss the pressures of structural sin on individual decisions, and to substitute speculative knowledge for inductive processes.

Feminist natural law sees human equality as essential to justice, although men and women may require some different preconditions of human flourishing. Like other liberation theologians, feminist theologians prioritize the welfare of society's most marginalized persons in defining and measuring justice. Attention to the realities of sin bring a committed search for forms of violence and oppression that can be hidden by apparently peaceful social order. Acknowledgment of sin and limits also leads to epistemological humility and self-criticism. Feminist natural law theorists also see the practical requirements of holistic flourishing, and therefore of virtue, varying according to person, time, and place. They will also employ the sciences to determine the conditions and varieties of human flourishing.

Feminism can accept the critical insight of post-modern thought that social power is an influence on all identities, beliefs, visions, and institutions. However, this insight cannot produce a constructive ethic. For this, a flexible and inductive vision of the good is required, built on knowledge about basic dimensions of human life and society, such as the human body, human development, health and disease, a well-functioning body politic, and environmental sustainability. Again, insights in all these areas are not only inductive and contextual, they are constantly evolving. Moreover, conflicts among goods and among the needs of persons and communities are unavoidable. Yet feminist theological natural law theory will persist in collaborative efforts toward ever greater realizations of welfare and political justice.

Maria Christina Astorga takes up the topics of human nature, natural law, and universality in ethics from the standpoint of an Asian discussion of 'human rights'. First, Astorga argues, following Brian Tierney and Jean Porter, that the concept of human rights is not a modern departure from natural law theory. It has roots in medieval Scholasticism. The medieval origin of human or natural rights is the idea that natural law is not limited to the ordering of communities. It includes the inherent faculty or ability of individual persons to act with relative liberty and autonomy, based on their powers of reason and moral discernment. The theological validation for this insight is the creation of humans in God's image.

A question today is why the doctrine of human rights, as conceived in a specific historical, cultural, and religious context, should be given validity across cultures and religions. This is a particularly pressing question in

Asia, with its immense diversity of culture, religions, economies, and political systems. The viability of human rights doctrine in Asia (and elsewhere) depends on a perspectival dialogue that aims to reach a compelling core of shared values, whose expression and codification will vary across cultures and worldviews.

The thrust of the 'Asian values' challenge to rights discourse is that Asia has an ethical model counter to the West, in that Asia values community over individual, social rights over civil and political rights, and social order and stability over democracy and freedom. This model also assumes a strong governing authority that functions interdependently with Asian values such as obedience, respect, industriousness, and emphasis on family. Critiques of this model include the ideas that Asia itself is diverse, that Asian governments have in fact acted provocatively, and that the values are more Confucian than universally Asian. Astorga adds that individual and community need not be so sharply contrasted, that the State at any rate cannot act on behalf of 'the community,' and that authoritarian regimes can act with impunity. She argues that civil and political rights are interdependent with economic and social rights. There is need for both universality and cultural specificity in defining human rights in Asia, as exemplified in the Philippine Bill of Rights.

Writing from an African perspective, Jacquineau Azetsop does not specifically take up the Western history of theories of natural law. Rather, he presents the concept of the vital life-force that grounds the African understanding of universal human existence, as well as an approach to morality that is life-centred and community-centred. This vital fore can be seen as an expression of natural law, since it is a force for progress in individual responsibility and social cohesion. But the determination of the concrete moral requirements of the life force unfolds communally, through the social discussion called 'palaver'. Palaver, as a means of moral discernment, reflects the African view of morality as focused on preservation of life and of social harmony.

For Africans, human fulfilment is not defined primarily in relation to the individual, but in relation to the web of relationships that constitute society, a web within which each member is also regarded as a subject in his or her own right. Yet African morality is not freedom-centred; it is a morality of virtue, responsibility, and communality in which the progress of the whole community is the goal. Azetsop fills in this picture with regard to health and illness. Disease is perceived not just as a biological phenomenon, but as a result of cosmic imbalances and disturbances of right relationships that the family and community must address. Thus the African approach to bioethics transcends the biomedical model. There is a close connection between the order of health and disease, the cosmic order and the moral order. Bioethics is not just about restoring physical function, it is about restoring right relationships. This approach coheres well with a model of disease in which the role of social inequities in creating poor health at the population level is emphasized.

Andrea Vicini comments on *The Search for a Universal Ethic*, the 2009 document of the International Theological Commission, which considers natural law to be an important asset in addressing international political and social issues. Vicini offers a summary of the document (which has been officially published only in French and Italian), and follows it with a critical discussion.

According to the ITC, reason can discover fundamental human inclinations that yield specific and objective moral precepts. These are not exclusively Christian, but can be found in all cultures and religions. Vicini sees the ITC approach as inductive, but incorporation of contemporary international authors would have been useful. Moreover, the ITC focuses its discussion and dialogue on social and political issues. But the use of natural law in magisterial teaching also includes bioethics and the ethics of sex and gender. Where is the inductive approach on these issues? The ITC affirms an objective universal ethic yet grants the cultural generation of specific ethical norms. What difference does this make at the practical level? Despite its limits, the document constitutes an invitation to dialogue with other traditions in the search for a universal ethic.

Kenneth Himes takes up a subject that presents an urgent test to the possibility of ethical universality: torture as 'an attack on the human'. Many people and societies seek an absolute ban on torture. What creates this strong opposition? Human beings share certain characteristics that lead to a minimal conception of the human good. Apprehensions about human rights are shared widely among cultures. Torture brings about negative consequences for individuals and communities. What is specifically wrong about torture is that it undermines personal integrity and even forces victims to collude in their own violation. Torture violates the essence of personhood in a more radical way even than killing.

Ivone Gebara examines the meaning of the term 'nature' from a feminist perspective to establish an approach to ecology. The Christian myth of divine creation 'from nothing' has contributed to a worldview in which God's superiority to nature and nature's dependence on God are imitated by human beings who dominate nature and so seek to know its laws in order to control it. The natural order, as willed by God, then becomes the basis for resistance to cultural change in the concept of the natural. In addition, a model of masculine rationality as 'power over' contributes to human exploitation of the planet. Finally, women are seen in naturalistic terms and as only secondarily rational. However, there remains a trace in different cultures, including Christianity, of an original feminine generative power and source of life. Various social movements and feminist philosophies and theologies reclaim this power, not to absolutize it, but to correct distorted patriarchal interpretations of God and nature. It is necessary to recognize the interdependence of all that exists, and to create a public politics of care for the poor, the stranger, the prisoner, the forests, and the rivers.

This issue concludes with a reflection by Hille Haker of a statement on the ethics of synthetic biology adopted by the European Group on Ethics of science and new technologies (EGE). Haker also presents the contents of the EGE opinion. Synthetic biology is the modification of existing organisms through the synthesis of artificial genes or proteins, metabolic or developmental pathways, and complete biological systems. There may be new applications in areas like drugs, food, biofuels, anti-pollutants, textiles, cosmetics, medical diagnostics, vaccines, and therapies. The concept of a stable and unchanging nature has already come into question with innovations in the life sciences such as genetic enhancement. Synthetic biology raises an even more dramatic question, because for the first time, change in the constitutive elements of life (including human life) is imaginable.

All these essays have in common an interest in critically reclaiming the moral realism of the natural law tradition, while at the same time recognizing its historical and cultural roots. The authors affirm human historicity and the inductive character of at least some aspects of ethical knowledge, as well as the essential role of the natural sciences in understanding humans and the entire natural world. Yet, in varying degrees and ways, all contributors also affirm the importance of making ethical judgments and forming ethical practices and institutions that conform to basic, non-relative norms of justice. A longstanding and continuing question about natural law is whether highly specific ethical norms can still be generalizable across cultures. A question for the future is whether 'natural law' will be the best framework and language for dialogue about the basic experiences, needs, goods, values, and goals that all human beings share.

Lisa Sowle Cahill with *Hille Haker*

The editors wish to thank Hilari Ragner (monk of Montserrat), Maria-Clara Bingemer, Erik Borgman, Elaine Wainwright, and M. Lamberigts for their help in preparing this issue.

Part One: Questions for Theology and Society

Tradition and Innovation in Natural Law:
A Thomistic Interpretation

STEPHEN J. POPE

Natural law is the primary traditional basis of Catholic ethics and politics, and Thomas Aquinas was its first and most influential architect. Thomistic natural law tradition went through major periods of intellectual development in the sixteenth, nineteenth, and twentieth centuries. The displacement of Thomism from the centre of Catholic thought in the wake of the Second Vatican Council was followed by a revival of interest in Thomistic natural law as well as virtue ethics.

The moral realism of Thomistic natural law gave it a capacity to assimilate insights that emerge from theology, philosophy, scientific theories, and new human experiences. After tracing the main lines of Thomas' account of natural law, this essay describes how Thomistic natural law has responded to the two major challenges in contemporary culture: cultural pluralism and evolutionary theory, respectively.

I. Thomas on natural law

Thomas Aquinas defined natural law as the rational creature's participation in the eternal law, the intelligent order that pervades all of creation. God, the unmoved mover and uncaused cause of every action, respects the inherent structure of nature and acts primarily in the world through 'secondary causes.'[1]

This is especially the case for moral agents, who are capable of directing their actions according to their own intelligent and free choices. The first point Thomas registers concerning law is that it is an ordering of acts by reason.[2] Reason operates in many ways and in different spheres, so it is necessary to understand the analogical uses of the term 'law'. Divine wisdom creates an ordered world, the eternal law in which animate and inanimate objects are moved to their good by the dynamism of their particular natures.

Human beings are unique in our ability to understand and voluntarily to direct our actions toward our end. The natural law is described as rational creature's 'participation' in the eternal law because we do so through the use of our own reason and simply by acting from instinct.[3] As unitary rational creatures composed of soul and matter, we are naturally inclined to seek external goods (such as wealth and good reputation), goods of the body (such as health and physical beauty), and goods of the soul (such as virtue and knowledge). We act in accord with the natural law when we pursue these kinds of goods in reasonable and responsible ways, and we violate the natural law when we act unreasonably and irresponsibly.

Because we are social creatures, our individual pursuit of these goods takes place in the context of community. Since the human good is common, the good life takes place in light of the common good and not just as a pursuit of one's private good. Natural law respects a proper balance between the love of self, family, and friends, and the social responsibility due to the wider community and especially its weakest members.

Every person has an inherent if general moral capacity to know that some acts are right and others wrong and everyone possesses an inclination to act in accord with what appears good to him or her at any particular point in time. The capacity has to be tutored and trained to take on a habit of the good or virtue. We are naturally inclined to want to know what is true, and though the human race as a whole tends to be cognitively underdeveloped and morally instable, we can, outside revelation and even outside of grace, come to some knowledge of the human good. We are capable of both acting to attain the goods 'connatural' to our nature such as building houses and planting vineyards[4] and capable of acquiring, by natural means of choice and habituation, the cardinal virtues of prudence, justice, temperance, and fortitude (though these virtues are not salvifically meritorious because they are not informed by charity).

The 'law' component of natural law, as noted above, concerns norms that govern the way we pursue the goods proper to our nature as human. Since every agent acts for an end that appears good, Thomas argued, we can see that good is the first thing that falls under the apprehension of practical reason (I-II, 94, 2). The 'first principle of practical reason' is thus founded on the notion of the good as that which all things seek. What Thomas calls 'the first precept of law,' to do good and avoid evil, is the basis of all the other precepts of the natural law. Because we are inclined to different kinds of goods – notably, physical, animal, and rational kinds of goods – the order of the norms of the natural law is coordinated with the order of the natural inclinations. In general, the well-lived life is ordered by reason, and, conversely, the disordered life is unreasonable. The virtues help to make reasonable judgments, choices, and acts a consistent feature of the morally developed person's life. A good community is one in which just institutions and strong bonds of civic friendship facilitate virtuous lives.

Positive law is the practical determination of how to promote this kind of good community in concrete circumstances. The authority for making law comes from either the whole people or someone who has care of the community.[5] The primary duty of political authority is to help citizens flourish, which includes protecting them from harm and helping them become good.[6] Yet there are limits to what positive law can be expected to accomplish. It should be expected neither to punish all vices nor to uphold a measure of virtue that it is impossible for the majority of citizens to obey. Laws that impose proportionate burdens bind the conscience of every citizen, all of whom benefit from living in a society governed by the rule of law.

II. Thomistic natural law and cultural pluralism

One major challenge to Thomistic natural law comes from our emerging knowledge of cultural pluralism. Thomas himself employed natural law when addressing pressing practical issues of his day such as the status of mendicant poverty, the buying and selling of credit, and the role of clerics in the waging of war. The substance of Thomas' ethic reflected his own particular culture, but the passage of time and the expansion of cultural context led to further developments.

Modern Thomists have appealed to natural law as correcting the narrow nationalism that automatically legitimates whatever is done in the name of the sovereign or the State, and as rejecting the moral voluntarism that justifies the right of the strong to dominate the weak. In the sixteenth century, theologians and lawyers at the University of Salamanca interpreted Thomistic natural law as lending support to the claim that all who share in the same human nature possess the same natural rights. The Salamancans used natural law, along with more distinctively theological and canonical legal arguments, to argue against the laws that justified the subjugation of the indigenous peoples of the Americas. This was taken to include rights to external goods such as property, bodily goods such as the right to life, and spiritual goods, such as the right to freedom of thought and the right to self-determination.

Francisco de Vitoria, O.P. (1492–1536), the 'father of international law', engaged in a creative re-interpretation of natural law ethics to include natural rights. Natural law justifies the right of every individual to own and control the goods necessary to sustain his or her life, and so justifies the freedom of indigenous people to maintain their own dominion free of Christian interference.[7] Bartolomé de Las Casas, O.P. (1474–1566), the 'Defender of the Indians,' took this argument a step farther in arguing that the indigenous communities have, according to just war doctrine, a right to defend themselves against unjust attacks from European colonial powers. Salamancan natural lawyers built on the criteria of just authority, just cause, and right intention, but they deemed as unjust wars waged to convert unbelievers or to gain territory.

The Salamanca school also employed natural law argumentation in the development of international law. They extended the primacy of the common good beyond the commonwealth to embrace the common good of all nations, a concept that later received much further development in Catholic social teachings.

In the twentieth century, natural law thinkers such as Jacques Maritain and John Courtney Murray, S.J., provided substantial argumentation, and in the face of some Catholic institutional resistance, to support liberal democracy and human rights. Natural law seeks a middle way between the two extremes of the tyranny of the majority and the anarchy of radical individualism. If the strength of liberal democracy lies in its appreciation of autonomy, self-reliance, diversity, tolerance, and difference, the strength of the natural law tradition resides in its attention to the social nature of the person and to our need for community, belonging, shared moral values, cooperation, solidarity, and the common good. Thomistic natural law appropriates the former while also respecting the special significance of the particular moral ties that bind local communities and insisting that all cultures dwell within a more overarching moral universe structured by human dignity and the human rights.

Thomistic natural law underscores what we most basically share as human beings, regardless of our religious differences. This perspective is especially important today, when religious divisions are so often the cause of conflict and violence around the world. Religion is of course the occasion of much goodness and peace, but particular religious loyalties are also easy to exploit and to turn against unbelievers.

Natural law theory recognizes the public dimension of morality. Its affirmation of the value of human intelligence encourages public conversation and consensus building. Its appreciation of the value of public reason expressed in language that allows everyone to be part of the same conversation affirms that people from diverse backgrounds have the capacity for reasoning together without ignoring the significance of ethnic or religious particularity. While religion provides the basis for cross-cultural identity for many people today, those who subscribe to natural law hold that religions, like States, should be held accountable to basic standards of decency, justice, and human rights.

Natural law respect for moral agency grounds the principle of subsidiarity and an appreciation for the moral significance of civil society. There are moral as well as legal and technical limits to state power, and society thrives best to the extent that the resources of a community are produced by a smoothly functioning civil society. Communities flourish only when civil society, State, and market are comprised of people who have learned civic virtues, especially civility, honesty, respect, and compassion.

III. Thomistic natural law and human evolution

A second major challenge to Thomistic natural law comes from Darwin and evolutionary accounts of human origins. Contemporary Thomistic natural law continues to affirm creation as ontologically dependent on God, but it can no longer regard the natural world as composed of a fixed hierarchy of species. Darwin's work and later scientific discoveries make it impossible to accept a literal interpretation of Genesis as a description of the origin of life on earth. Darwin's theory of 'descent with modification', or 'natural selection', depicts human beings as intelligent animals who evolved under the same pressures to survive and reproduce that shaped all other species. Darwin focused on the continuities that humans share with other animals, understood intelligence and emotions as generally evolved to serve fitness, and regarded human sociality and cooperation as derivative from competition and conflict. Instead of essences, Darwin saw nature in terms of populations marked by variations; instead of formal and final causes, he was concerned with the effect of material and efficient causes on human behaviour.

The Thomistic natural law tradition has made an ambivalent response to Darwin and the theories of evolution that followed him. The first response tends to be a negative assessment of ideologies that have used Darwinian evolution to legitimate reactionary social policies. Darwin's own analysis of

the evolutionary process was deeply dependent on Thomas Malthus' claim
that conditions of scarcity tend to 'cull' the weakest members of a population
(in Darwin's terms, 'unfavorable variations'). Social Darwinians concluded
that inhibiting the natural elimination of the unfit in the long run adds to
human misery. Social Darwinians regarded the ruthlessness of nature as a
normative model for social policy, but Darwin himself believed that human
sympathy could not tolerate callous disregard of the weakest.

Natural law theorists thus do well to draw a clear line between scientific
findings proper and normative extrapolations purportedly based on them.
Natural law ethics is open to the former while strongly opposing the latter,
particularly its reductionism, ontological naturalism, and moral determin-
ism. Natural law provides a philosophically-grounded moral framework
within which relevant findings of science can be properly assimilated while
also resisting its ideological misuses.

The second Thomistic response, critical appropriation of evolutionary
science, is based on the claim of moral realism that truth cannot ultimately
be opposed to truth. We can no longer engage in ethics with an anthropology
that assumes that we are cultural beings but not biological beings whose bio-
gram reflects a long evolutionary history. Natural law theories once assumed
that we live on a planet that is 10,000 years old, that our remote ancestors
once dwelled in a primeval paradise, and that we have for all time existed
at the centre of the universe. None of these once-believed claims can be
affirmed as true today.

The Thomistic natural law tradition can only be intellectually viable today
if it is developed on the basis of an evolutionary theism that holds that the
Creator has employed billions of years of biological evolution as the means
for producing creatures capable of loving and knowing. Evolution as a process of 'emergent complexity' employs terms like 'finality', 'purpose', and
'design' in a way that takes into account the role of 'chance and necessity' in
the working of evolution.

Evolutionary theory provides an account of the biological reasons for why
we are naturally oriented to certain kinds of goods, most obviously bodily
goods (longevity, good appearance, sense pleasure, etc.) and external goods
(wealth, honour, fame, power) but also, at least in some respects, Thomas'
'goods of the soul' (including intellectual ability, knowledge, and friendship). Human nature has been slowly shaped over millions of years to have
traits that, singly or in combination, as adaptive or by-products of adaptive
traits, contributed to reproductive fitness. Human intelligence, including
culture, can shape and guide biologically-rooted human traits but they do

not completely over-ride them. Natural law theory suggests that while our species shares the same evolutionary ordering to fitness as other species, our emergent social, emotional, and cognitive capacities can allow our conduct to serve higher purposes than reproduction. Emergent human complexity has led us to a nature that can find higher meaning and more profound purpose in the love of God and love of neighbour.

Thomistic natural law developed in an evolutionary context seeks an appropriate flexibility in its understanding of human nature and is open to the complexities of the human good, because it understands our traits as themselves the product of both a complex and uneven evolutionary process, not as the product of a simple and straightforward blueprint of the kind envisioned by the 'Intelligent Design' movement. Natural law theory informed by evolutionary biology can appreciate the diversity within human populations in a way that older conceptions did not. In focusing on the concrete human good available for particular individuals and their communities, not what is good 'for man' in the abstract, it can recognize that the moral ideal for some people might be unattainable for others.

Evolutionary considerations also highlight the potential for conflict as well as the harmony that can mark both internal human subjectivity and external social relations. Human traits did not evolve according to a pre-ordained internal harmony. Underscoring the importance of the virtues for responding to concrete goods in the right way, contemporary natural law theory gives special emphasis on the importance of the virtue of prudence in determining the most responsible way of living for each person.

Concluding reflections

At its best, natural law in the Thomistic tradition conserves Thomas' moral realism and integral view of the human good while also being inspired by modern and contemporary insights into the evolved basis of this good and its communal and cultural context.

Thomistic natural law is known for providing an alternative to moral scepticism and moral relativism. Moral scepticism often makes the ontological claim that there is no 'moral structure' to reality and/or the epistemological claim that, even if there were a moral order, we are not competent to discover it. Moral relativism holds that normative judgments are nothing but the prejudices of particular groups or traditions. Natural law ethics, on the other hand, is committed to three contrary affirmations: that there is a moral order intrinsic to reality; that practical reason, when it functions properly, can yield knowledge of what is right and good both in a general sense and in concrete circumstances; and that there are moral truths, including human rights, that transcend cultural boundaries and include every human community.

These moral truths are rooted in human nature as it has been created by God through the process of evolution: that we have an inherent dignity rooted in our capacity to understand and to love, that we flourish by attaining certain goods in community, and that we take responsibility for one another and for ourselves. Incorporation of an evolutionary, culturally pluralistic context leads us to interpret natural law in a dynamic, flexible, and comprehensive way.

The future shape of Thomistic natural law depends on how it responds to two profound practical challenges from the contemporary world. First, the greatest challenge to natural law over the course of the last half-century or so concerns the ethics of sex and gender. We are increasingly alert to the danger of confusing nature with culture and of making normative values that are in fact culturally contingent biases and value judgments. Greater knowledge of how culture shapes our perception of human nature and of diversities across as well as within particular cultures have discredited the stereotypes and rigid gender roles that were once assumed to be permanently fixed in human nature. If natural law supports the equal dignity and moral agency of all human beings, then male domination has to be regarded as a violation of the natural law rather than its proper expression.[8]

Second, Thomistic natural law faces a new challenge in developing an ecological ethic to complement its social ethic. Our deepening knowledge of the strain under which the natural world now operates, and our recognition of the earth as our natural habitat (and not just a temporary and disposable abode), inspires a much more serious concern with ecological ethics than has marked natural law theories in the past. Our growing awareness of how much of our social, cognitive, and emotional functioning is shared in common with other animals underscores the embodied character of moral and social responsibility. A new emphasis on the *natural* context of natural law provides a vantage point from which to critique the widespread abuse of nature and to insist that we accept the full scope and depth of our ecological responsibilities. Just as the Salamancans expanded the common good from the commonwealth to the international community, so today ecological natural law must expand our awareness of the common good to include the earth. In calling for a greater commitment to care for nature itself, Thomistic natural law must thus learn how to advocate ecologically responsible Christian human-ism without continuing in the now discredited tradition of Christian anthropocentrism.[9]

Notes

1. See Brian Tierney, *The Idea of Natural Rights*, Grand Rapids: Eerdmans, 1997, pp. 262–5.
2. See Thomas Aquinas, *Summa theologiae* I, q.105.
3. ST I–II, q.90, a.1.
4. I–II, q.91, a.2.
5. I–II, q.109, aa. 2, 5.
6. I–II, q.90, a.3.
7. I–II, q.92, a.1.
8. See Cristina L. H. Traina, *Feminist Ethics and Natural Law: The End of Anathemas*, Washington, D.C.: Georgetown University Press, 1999.
9. See Michael S. Northcott, *The Environment and Christian Ethics*, New York: Cambridge University Press, 1996, esp. ch. 7.

Natural Law and Theology in a Secular Context

ANDRÉS TORRES QUEIRUGA

It is commonplace to state that the 'natural law' can embrace everything: from revolutionary impulse to absolutist restraint. Many people see it as a generic preamble, changeable according to one's own interests, and others as such a multi-sided concept as to be meaningless. Its long history is a contributory factor here. Specifically, modern secularization signifies a radical shift in outlook that requires a new understanding, of both the concept itself and the effect it has on theology. In a search for this new understanding, I shall take account of the change in *epistemological* outlook, with its ethical consequences, and in the concept of *revelation*, with its repercussion on the relationship between ethics and magisterium (using the terms 'morals' and 'ethics' indiscriminately in what follows).

I. Traditional experience: a secular view

The experience of an underlying order ruling reality, such as *maat*, *rita*, *tao*, or *logos*, is present in all cultures. Despite its numerous deficiencies, nature is perceived as a cosmos and not as a chaos. Human beings order their lives rightly by adapting to it or following it. Just as we cannot eat everything, because our 'biological nature' prevents us from doing so, neither can we behave in whatever fashion we choose, because our 'social nature' requires norms that make right behaviour feasible. Stoicism, given currency in the Roman world by Cicero, expressed the basic idea: living in accordance with *nature* equally means living according to the *logos*; ethical norms and civic laws are concrete expressions of this law. Platonism, with its exemplarism, said basically the same thing. Christianity inherited this view, accentuating the personalism characteristic of biblical revelation. And Scholasticism, with Thomas Aquinas especially, organized it into a system that still profoundly influences theology.

It may seem otiose to recall this process, but it needed doing in order to situate the radical change of direction brought about by Modernity. This has two basic aspects: (1) secularization broke the derivation – till then seen as self-evident and indissoluble – of human law from divine law: *etsi Deus non daretur*; (2) biblical criticism changed the concept of revelation: God did not 'dictate' the commandments. Failure to pay sufficient attention to these changes is producing confusion. The solution cannot lie in 're-touching' St Thomas: studies that show his richness and potentiality are useful and perhaps necessary, but his thought belongs to the pre-secular paradigm. The change is not one of shading or detail but is a re-working of the whole picture. We now need a fresh overall look at the problem, one that will frame it in secularized culture.

I shall try to clarify this through recourse to the analysis made by Ángel Amor Ruibal (from Santiago de Compostela; d. 1930), a thinker as unknown as he was brilliant. After a thorough survey of classical theology, considered in its interactions with philosophy, he (deeply concerned with the Modernist question and seeking a profound renewal in theology) accepts that its achievement was 'as great as it could then have been'; his general diagnosis, however, was: '[N]ot only must we no longer return to the incoherent and artificial syncretism of contrasting philosophical ideas [. . .], with the no less artificial and unavoidable alternative of Plato and Aristotle, but *we now need a deep transformation of the theory of being and knowing*, starting with the latter'.[1]

Applying this to the present concern points to the need for moving beyond the 'Platonic exemplarism' that – concealed or overt – forms the inner structure that informs the traditional interpretation, imposing a descent by degrees, so that, just as Plato saw things reflecting 'ideas', the *eternal law* becomes the exemplar of the *natural law*. This establishes a fundamentally deductive reasoning, the result of which is to make natural law a reflection of the immutability, universality, and intangibility of eternal law.

His analysis is far more detailed,[2] but his emphasis lies in denouncing the *inversion* of the true process, since 'natural law (and the moral conscience built on it) should not be considered as the copy of an abstract type in ourselves, whereas it is the other way round: the abstract type is of our own devising, derived from the plan of nature presented to our perception in the world around us' (342). In other words, what looked like a copy of a perfect and eternal divine model is shown to be human deduction, tentative and progressive. He thus introduces a realist interpretation, which leads directly to reflection in a secular context, because it is in the world such as it is, even 'without thinking of the Divinity, without regarding either the universe or oneself as God's work' (341), that we have to read the moral values that lie at the root of the law.

II. Realism at root and flexibility in interpretation

This radical shift in outlook defines the current situation. In the first place, we see that in ethics or morals, precisely, we should not speak of '*natural law*' but of '*human* laws' that interpret natural dynamisms, whose real ethical meaning we have to discover ourselves. This needs stressing, because language is not innocent. Given the intensity of consciousness of *evolution* our culture has acquired and, above all, of *historicity* in human affairs, there are no such things as fixed laws, as evident 'scripture', but only relationship and dynamisms we have to decipher and which are constitutively open-ended, constantly adapted to new situations. This has two decisive outcomes:

(1) Speaking of 'natural law' can only refer to human norms dealing with fundamental dynamisms capable of showing themselves as requirements to be genuinely worked out by each of us, in whatever situation. But merely making such a statement demonstrates our distance from that easy certainty with which the ancients – down to the pioneers of the Enlightenment –were able to speak of evident and universal natural precepts.

(2) This raises the problem of upholding, on the one hand, the *objective basis* of norms, against all voluntarism or juridical positivism, and, on the other, of accepting their *historical variability* in the face of any and every objectivist absolutism. This is possible (despite any accusation of 'naturalist fallacy') thanks to the specific and irreducible character of ethical intentionality. This is because ethics pertains to the primordial experiences, which Phenomenology (remember the 'principle of all principles') has shown as legitimizing themselves in their self-presentation. But what happens is that, placed at the level of *pre-comprehension*, such experiences never appear in pure form, as separate concepts, but as 'instances' included in actual concepts. This can only be understood through a bi-level dialectic: what is *transcendental* in the experiences and what is *categorial* in actual concretions.

This is a difficult dialectic, especially in the order of feeling and will, to which ethics belongs. This is why Ricoeur recommends explaining it with the aid of 'cognoscitive intentionality', which is always clearer.[3] So, then speaking of *being*, Amor Ruibal states that this is not a 'concept' but a 'notion', meaning an experience that is primordial, a-thematic, totally universal, and undefined. As such, it cannot exist in a pure form (a 'being-as-being' does not exist), but simply for this reason it can take shape as an 'instance' included in any concept (all that is known 'is'). With regard to the notion of being, he goes on to study 'second notions' or 'notional categories', such as 'life' or 'consciousness'. These represent vectors of the dynamism of a being that, when they appear, situate it and qualify it but do not determine specific embodiments; this is why they can come about as 'instances' in ever-new concretions without any *a-prioric* limits: vegetable-life, animal-life, divine-life (the same *notional* value contained in different *concepts*).[4]

Applying this to knowledge of God, Amor Ruibal displays both realism and flexibility: 'We have here on one hand the possibility that human concepts can express something with respect to God, translating notional values of being and of those perfections as *something absolute*; on the other, the impossibility of ideas being able to express, except proportionately and keeping *infinite distances* apart, the greatness of God through the littleness of creatures and their representations.'[5]

There is no doubt that applying the same dialectic to ethical intentionality proves illuminating. So it is significant that Maritain, though dealing with a different context, should speak in almost identical terms of primordial moral regulations as 'simple forms or general tendential frameworks, [. . .] *dynamic schemes* of moral rules, corresponding to that which primordial or 'primitive' notions of understanding by inclination are capable of, in their first flush.'[6]

The disputed question of whether 'intrinsic evil' exists or not is thereby given a solution that is both realist *and* flexible. Dealing with arbitrary voluntarism, Amor Ruibal states that an 'organic concept of the world' makes it logical for 'the norms of natural law to impose themselves on the spirit, in more or less defined ways [. . .], in the manner that the laws of physical nature automatically impose themselves in their respective category' (354). But this very realism at the basic level excludes any absolutism in specific applications, since 'the relative nature of the order of creation can do no less than make the concept of natural rights and duties equally relative' (*ibid.*). Just as in the order of being, so too in that of duty there exists only the formal *immutability* of the principle of non-contradiction: to do good and avoid evil (340). Everything else is subordinated to the radical contingency of *this* creation and to the historical variation in norms shown by our freedom to respond to the dynamisms best suited to genuine human self-fulfilment.

In specific terms: the fundamental moral requirement always remains *intrinsically* valid: we should do good and avoid evil – breaking this rule would amount to contradicting our own ethical intentionality. The *primary values* with which this intentionality is concerned, such as respect for life or recognition of equality, remain equally valid. But here absoluteness refers only to their 'notional value', not to all their specific embodiments, which are now 'conceptual' interpretations and can vary in differing circumstances: defending innocent-life may involve eliminating criminal-life.

This does not imply relativism, since the *objective* notional value stands, and this refers us back to reality by which to measure the morality of its execution. In identical circumstances the decision that best embodies the notional value is the *only* morally correct one. Friedo Ricken formalizes this neatly: taking p and q as the circumstances and ϕ as the decision, a universal deontic judgment should be: 'Everyone that is *exclusively* affected by p and q should make ϕ'.[7]

In reality, far from implying relativism, the only thing this excludes is abstract a-priorism, since it shows that *every actual decision* is intrinsically good or evil, as otherwise it would be contradictory: 'Precisely because moral values represent a metaphysical value, they need to be subordinated to the principle of contradiction when they are embodied in a given order of ethical relationships' (346).[8]

III. The autonomy of morality

From Plato's *Eutriphon* and the traditional 'mandated because it is good', the inductive view of ethics as discovery of the values inscribed in natural dynamisms has always been present. But as effective evidence it has imposed itself on the basis of the Enlightenment's *etsi Deus non daretur*. It was good that this was formulated by the Christian Grotius, to demonstrate that the formula is not atheist *in itself* but reflects faith in *creation* as something made available to *human* understanding and freedom. It was in fact a logical expression of the *autonomy* of creation, solemnly proclaimed by Vatican II, not only for 'material being' but for society itself: 'If by the autonomy of earthly affairs is meant the gradual discovery, utilization and ordering of the laws and values of matter and society, then the demand for autonomy is perfectly in order: it is at once the claim of humankind today and the desire of the creator' (GS 36).

It was initially difficult to draw the consequences, even for *science*, as the conflicts with Galileo and Darwin showed. But today the case is made: there is no 'religious' astronomy or biology. And, furthermore, we appreciate the *religious* gain from understanding that the Bible is not a book of science. The same needs to happen with morals. They are equally founded in creation, and discovering their laws is a human undertaking: this requires no distinction between atheists and believers; it rather demands a common quest for common results. This is what is meant by *the autonomy of morality*.

Where *contents* are concerned, and however strange it might seem at first, we need to draw the consequences: (1) just as is true of astronomy, there is no 'religious morality' either: on principle, Christians and atheists have no reason to follow different norms; (2) the Bible is not a book of morality, any more than it is of astronomy or biology. The direct object of *revelation* is not moral directives, any more than it was Joshua's astronomy, but *motivation* as a divine call and an aid to carrying out these directives. God did not 'dictate' the commandments to Moses (who was so influenced by his surroundings) and Paul adopted Stoic ethics. But both exhorted their fulfilment.

Nevertheless, the achievements of science have not (yet) been so easy for morals to accept: in fact, as Alfons Auer has pointed out, official Catholic documents 'essentially uphold the traditional conception'.[9] This is understandable: on the one hand, such a profound change in traditional habits raises the fear of de-authorizing the Church and abandoning morality; on the other, it is clear that – without denying the parallelism – it would be simplistic to ignore the difference, since religious experience has an indissoluble link with morality.

This is why it is absolutely necessary to draw the *basic distinction between contents and motivation*. The earlier statement needs completing: there is no 'religious morality', but there is *a religious way of living morality*.[10] Religion does not dictate the contents, but it does set them in a specific context and provide a particular ground for their fulfilment. There is nothing written anywhere, including in the Bible, to establish whether a cloning is morally good. This is a task to be undertaken by human beings working together in an inter-disciplinary dialogue that calibrates processes, objectives, and consequences. But knowing *what* morality is does not simply equate to acting morally: any tax evader or even rapist knows this full well. Each world-view motivates and establishes its fulfilment in a different way.

IV. The role of religion in morality

As happened with science, what may look like a loss in fact represents a gain: it simply requires a re-formulation of the manner of presence. Even *where the contents are concerned*, it does not mean abandoning them but entering squarely into the common dialogue. What is new is recognizing the difference between *discovery* and *justification*: the reasons for a moral norm have to be grounded within its own intentionality. Habermas is right to insist that in public discourse even ethical truths discovered *in* a religious context have to be *argued* ethically.

This is why the Church cannot monopolize interpretation of the (so-called) 'natural law'. To say so is not to do away with its influence. As the historical matrix of many moral discoveries, religion has an enormous store of wealth to contribute: to exclude it from public debate would prove a great loss. What concerns us is avoidance of polemic and its replacement with dialogue: contributing and learning. There are, for example, aspects such as equality, the absolute value of the person, or forgiveness, that can be more clearly grasped through confessing God as 'Father-Mother'. But religion can also learn: remitting to the Absolute, which makes it especially sensitive to some issues, can make it blinder to others, as the resistance to toleration or freedom of conscience shown by the nineteenth-century magisterium demonstrated.

In any case, *the direct and specific relationship with ethics* is situated on the level of motivation.[11] We cannot believe in a God-love and fail to treat all men and women as brothers and sisters. We might even state that the 'commandment to love' forms the Christian version of Kant's *faktum morale*. Here the religion–ethics link is not only direct and indissoluble; it also enables us to recover its true meaning.

Conceiving morality as revelation of contents effectively led to it being seen as an obligation imposed from outside, very focused on 'God's rights' and those of the Church as well. It thereby induced a heteronomous view of moral motivation, focused on hope of reward and fear of punishment. The interest of religion and human interests seemed to be opposed and irreconcilable: what was good for us would not always be good for God, and God's will tended to be seen as imposition, threat, or even denial of humanity. The result was to hide the genuine meaning of religious insistence on morality: to encourage and support authentic human self-fulfilment.

The distinction allows us to recover the primary meaning. The God-who-creates-by-love seeks nothing for himself, but solely and exclusively the good of his creatures. His glory is 'the living human being' (Ireneaus), and we do not offend God 'except when we act against our own good' (Thomas Aquinas). Despite all its distortions in history, the Christian moral position is that whatever is good for us is good for God: any human progress, in the cultural sphere as in the social, in scientific endeavour as in food production or world peace, is at one and same time a prolongation of God's creating and saving action.[12]

Just like the forced renunciation of the Papal States, so too acceptance of autonomy in contents allows the Church to concentrate on its specific mission: to encourage and support the observance of those ethical models that *as human beings* we progressively find to be the best. Its initial resistance to signing the Declaration on Human Rights because it did not mention God failed to take this distinction into account; this is why the decision could be changed: the Declaration affects *contents*; the Church has the right to uphold its specific *motivation*.

V. Magisterium and ethical dialogue

Actual problems pose a different question. Clarity of principle often clashes with the difficulty in agreeing on contents, since ethics also suffers from the 'conflict of interpretations'. In itself, this pluralism is intrinsic to ethics; it does not breach the faith-unbelief frontier. But what can – and does – come about is that the Church judges a particular content to be so intimately linked to God as its motivating ground that it cannot accept its negation. Such a case was its opposition to infanticide, mentioned as early as the Letter to Diognetus.

Unfortunately, not all cases are as clear as this. So it is *in this area* that the real problems surface, and then only realist and respectful dialogue suffices. The Church has to show itself true to religious intentionality and build on its long historical experience, using it as a source of enlightenment but also as a source of caution, distinguishing carefully between contents and motivation. Modern blunders over the former show the need for an adaptation of attitudes that, under the guise of 'religious' conclusions, can be mere *cultural* legacy, no longer valid today. The case of *Humanae Vitae* has become a paradigmatic warning.

Caution in regard to the *indirect* relationship with contents and concentration on the *direct* relationship with motivations would increase the Church's credibility. Accepting itself as a companion in dialogue, without claiming to have *always and already* the solution to problems as new as those that have arisen in bioethics, new sexuality, equality of women, or the distribution of the world's wealth, far from diminishing its prestige, would increase its authority. Allowing itself to be also 'disciple' in the new fields of human knowledge would facilitate its recognition as a 'Master in Humanity' from its specific viewpoint. This is in fact an especially fertile field for ethical dialogue with modern culture. Here are three points that would deserve a detailed exposition:

(1) The difficulty in finding the right solution to new problems would thus be shown to be a universal human problem, which can be resolved only on grounds of the common good, not as a struggle for partisan concerns or a debate between 'progressivism' and religion. Very serious questions such as abortion or birth-rate would without any doubt benefit from this approach.

(2) The specific contribution religion can make to the *ultimate* grounding of ethical motivation would emerge clearly. Freud, asking himself why one should act morally if this was to one's own disadvantage, recognized: 'I have not been capable of answering myself, which is far from reasonable'.[13] Horkheimer insisted tirelessly that the answer can be found only from an absolute basis.[14] And Habermas himself states: 'On this point it might perhaps be said that it is useless to try to preserve an unconditional meaning without God.'[15] As a contributor to dialogue, without claiming a monopoly, religion has an undoubtedly fruitful opening here.

(3) Finally – and perhaps most importantly – we would do away with a misunderstanding that, in my view, is damaging the dialogue between philosophy and religion. Religious respect for ethical intentionality equally points to the need for ethical-philosophical respect for religious intentionality; without this, no clarification is possible. The conversation between Marcel Gauchet and Luc Ferry alerted me to this point.[16] Both agree on affirming the experiential persistence of the religious sense; Ferry also upholds, against Gauchet, that religious values are *irreducible*, but he has problems in founding this on a '*transcendence in immanence*', which tends to fall back into the purely ethical realm.

The same can be seen in Habermas. In his last publication he recognizes the 'surprising continuity' of his thinking on the subject, positing a 'methodical frontier between faith and knowledge'.[17] He admits he was, like Weber, too ready to proclaim 'the privatization of the potentialities of faith (*Galubensmächten*) and its absorption 'into the profane principles of a universalist ethics'.[18] Above all, however, he always focuses discussion on ethical-political valency. This, to my mind, makes a true meeting impossible, because, as happens with scientism, the usual reductionist dialectic reappears: the more ethics progresses, the more religion recedes; in the end it will fade away to nothing. In Spain, J. A. Marina expressed this clearly: born of religion, ethics will be its 'parricidal offspring'.[19]

Religion's tough apprenticeship in respect for the autonomy of science and ethics can today sound a call for them to respect its own. This would be an all-round gain to the benefit of humanity.

Translated by Paul Burns

Notes

1. A. Amor Ruibal, *Los problemas fundamentales de la Filosofía y el Dogma*, 12 vols, Santiago, I–VI, 1914–21; VII–X, 1933–6; I cite the new edition, vol. IV,

Santiago, 2000, p.227 (page refs. henceforward in text).

2. Cf. *op. cit.*, II, pp. 295–360; also J. M. Caamaño, 'Necesidad y libertad. La ley natural en la obra de Ángel Amor Ruibal', *Estudios Eclesiásticos* 320 (2007), 39–83.

3. See *L'homme faillible*, Paris, 1960, pp. 99–104.

4. The small point-size is intended to suggest this character of a-thematic 'instances'. I clarify this in 'Dieu comme "personne" d'après la dialectique notion-concept chez Amor Ruibal', in M. Olivetti (ed.), *Intersubjectivité et théologie philosophique* (Archivio di Filosofia), Padua, 2001, pp. 699–712.

5. Unpublished text; my italics.

6. *El hombre y el estado* (1953), Madrid, 1983, pp. 110–11.

7. *Ética general*, Barcelona, 1987, p. 177, n. 91.

8. Finally, the International Theological Commission also accepted this in 1980: 'Indeed, all sin is *contra natura* insofar as it is opposed to right reason and hinders the authentic development of the human person' (n. 80).

9. *Autonome Moral und christlicher Glaube*, Düsseldorf ²1984, p. 160; cf. 160–3.

10. I have studied this in 'Moral e relixión: da moral relixiosa á visión relixiosa de moral', *Encrucillada* 28/136 (2004), 5–24 (Sp. trans. and synthesis in *Selecciones de Teología* 4 [2005], 83–92).

11. This already happens with ethical *intentionality*. The idea of creation as a free decision by God for the good of humankind shows that reality is *in itself* called to ethical fulfilment, thereby opposing itself to the positivist claim of an 'axiological neutrality' that would accede to ethics only through the naturalist fallacy.

12. This is magnificently expressed in the concept of *theonomy*, as 'autonomous reason united to its own profundity' (P. Tillich, *Systematic Theology*, 3 vols, Chicago, 1951–63; here Sp. trans., *Teología Sistemática*, Barcelona, 1972, p. 116). Seeing reality as creation-out-of-love, theonomy synthesizes autonomy and heteronomy, so that the same moral action can be expressed in two different linguistic games: as good for human beings, in the secular game; as the will of God, in the religious.

13. Letter to J. Putnam, 8 July 1915, in *Epistolario 1873–1939*, Madrid, 1963, p. 347.

14. 'What depends on morality rests, in the final analysis, on theology, despite the prudence we should exercise in conceiving it' (*Zur Kritik der instrumentellen Vernunft*, Frankfurt, 1974, p. 247 and *passim*).

15. *Textos y Contextos*, Barcelona, 1996, p. 147.

16. *Le religieux après la religion*, Paris, 2004.

17. *Philosophische Texte 5*, Frankfurt, 2009, p. 32.

18. *Ibid.*, p. 433.

19. Cf. A. Torres Queiruga, 'Ética y religion: ¿"vástago parricida" o hija emancipada?', *Razón y Fe* 249/1266 (2004), 295–314.

A Kantian Approach to the Natural-Law Theory of Aquinas

EBERHARD SCHOCKENHOFF

The concept of 'natural-law' ethics in the tradition of Catholic moral theology refers to a cognitive moral theory that maintains the truthfulness and universal applicability of moral judgments. Its normative pronouncements do not depend on human emotional assertions (emotivity), or on intentional valuation (value philosophy), or on the wholly procedural processes of an inter-subjective reason (discursive ethics). Instead the theory of natural law (*lex naturalis*) refers to a pre-given objective basis already available in the nature of human beings and in the existential goals that inhere in them as part of that very nature. In modern ethics, however, this fundamental assumption is the focus of a number of critical objections, which must be taken into account by an attempt to re-establish the natural-law theory of Thomas Aquinas on a transcendental basis.

An argument that inquires into the relevance of the natural for the conduct of individual human lives and the normative order of their communal existence must link the principles of an ethical life and a legal order to the specific character of a nature shared by all human beings. Neo-Scholastic teachings on natural law took it for granted that the nature common to all humans was an ascertainable fixed value with a clearly determinable extent, content and normative relevance. This assumption indicates a fundamental difficulty of attempts to define natural-law ethical systems, since the term 'nature' in itself is never unambiguous. It requires a thoroughgoing distinction to be made between the inescapable minimum conditions that are to be taken as transcendental presuppositions of being moral subjects and the more responsible conceptions of the good life that are an essential part of the personal identity of each individual.

I. The notion of 'natural life'

At first the hint of an etymological explanation offered by the basic meaning of the word 'nature' (from the past participle of the Latin *nasci* = to be born) tells us nothing about the permanent existential order that is an inalienable part of the essential nature of all human beings. But when the concept of nature is interpreted in the light of the paradisiacal myth of an aboriginal, virgin state of things, the notion of a 'natural life' becomes a formula that can be invoked by a whole range of different viewpoints. They extend from a pessimistic, retrograde analysis of the contemporary situation to futuristic social utopias that have profoundly influenced the socio-political history of ideas of the modern era. A good example of proponents of the first possibility would be Seneca, the philosopher of classical antiquity who categorized all the achievements of the civilization of his time, from house-building, agriculture, and cattle rearing, through crafts and art, all the way to landowning and private property, as 'unnatural' ways of life into which the Roman people had descended by abandoning the prosperous circumstances of earlier times.[1] An instance of the utopian variant is to be found at the end of the *Ancien Régime* in France in Rousseau's *Du contrat social* (Social Contract) of 1762. There an idyllic Arcadian nature fits the blithe, relaxed mood of free citizens who, in accordance with the fiction of the social contract, and in a fundamental act constitutive of civic society, confirm their individual rights (in particular the right to personal security and private property) for all ages thereafter.[2]

A similar contradiction is apparent in the ethics of antiquity, for the Stoics appealed to nature and rejected precisely what the Epicurean philosophers had recommended as a way of life that accorded with nature and promoted physical and psychic well-being. Whereas the Epicureans saw human beings in terms of their empirical nature as creatures of needs and urges, the Stoic moralists tried to use spiritual exercises to train humans to assert the rule of reason over the world of their inclinations and passions, and thereby to acknowledge their specific determination as human.[3] This contradiction between humankind as an empirical nature of needs and urges and humanity as an ideal nature of reason, which recurs as a radical dichotomy in Kant's ethics in the modern era, indicates a primary fundamental alternative which all theories of natural law have to confront.

II. The teleological interpretation of nature

A third possibility, which became especially significant in the Aristotelian-Thomist tradition, considers humans in their body-soul identity and interprets them as vital intellectual and physical beings subject to the primacy of reason. This conception became available to philosophy once Aristotle had transformed the *a priori* intuition of the Platonic theory of ideas into a teleological metaphysics. Then the idea of natural law can be set in an interpretation of the world affording material implications for all areas of reality. According to the basic principles of the Aristotelian view of nature, every living being has a form that accords with its essential nature, is established in the material substrate of its potential, and is implemented in a goal-directed developmental process. In the case of animals and plants, this process is consonant with their organic growth, in the course of which they reach their own particular entelechy, or mode of being when their essence is completely realized. In humans, the species-specific determination of their nature, that is, their specific *telos*, includes the development of their reason, which is part of what humans are essentially intended to be. The 'purpose' of a determinate being always denotes the development of its nature to the ultimate extent of its potentiality, when the Aristotelian accordance with nature is no longer conceived of as the original but as the fully achieved state in the sense of the best possible state of a thing or living being.

Aquinas argues on this basis when defining what is human: 'Now in human actions, good and evil are predicated in reference to the reason . . . the good of [humankind] is to be in accordance with reason [*secundum rationem esse*], and evil is to be against reason [*praeter rationem*]. For that is good for a thing which suits it in regard to its form; and evil, that which is against the order of its form'.[4] Accordingly, the natural is the rational, a fulfilment established in the natural aims of human striving, or natural inclinations (*inclinationes naturales*), which the practical reason sees as developing the powers that belong to human beings as part of their very nature. In accordance with the axiom *bonum habet rationem finis* (the good has the character of a goal), the practical reason apprehends the good as a potential for fulfilment inherent in human existence and in natural human striving, aiming at the identity of humanity, sentience (sensuousness) and reason.[5] The practical reason does not command the natural inclinations from without by suppressing them, as happens with controlled individuals whose emotions succumb to the mastery of reason. It develops instead *in* natural inclinations; *in* a desire for self-preservation and procreation, for recognition and love, and for friendship and community; and, finally, *in* striving to know the truth; and does so in order to lead these natural tendencies to the *optimum potentiae*, the ultimate possibility of human capabilities. The *inclinationes naturales* accord with natural law only as effort shaped by reason, just as morally inappropriate behaviour arises from the passions refusing to be integrated by reason ('. . . good is the first thing that falls under the apprehension of the practical reason, which is directed to action; since every agent acts for an end under the aspect of good, viz., that good is that which all things seek after. . . . Since . . . good has the nature of an end, and evil the nature of a contrary, hence it is that all those things to which [humankind] has a natural inclination, are naturally apprehended as being good, and consequently as objects of pursuit, and their contraries as evil, and objects of avoidance').[6]

III. What is good for humanity

The standard objection to natural law does not apply to an ethics that defines the good as that which accords with reason, and as the ultimate existential accomplishment of fundamental human capabilities. Then human 'nature' is no longer conceived of in the sense of a static order of being of the kind presupposed by the natural-law ethics of neo-Scholasticism. Instead an essentially appropriate human nature should be interpreted as an ensemble of inherent dynamic opportunities for development, which individually responsible human action is intended to put into practice. If the morally good is conceived of along these lines as the destined goal of a developmental process that puts into effect latent capacities of the human form of existence, the 'naturalistic fallacy' can be dismissed as irrelevant. In fact, on this assumption there is no dichotomy between mere facts and the moral values that might be ascribed to them from without. After all, the good and valuable – reaching the goal – is established in the nature of a determinate being. The good is always the fully accomplished state of an entity, and in the case of human beings the good is a rationally accordant existence that fulfils the highest potentials of the human form of life. In our contemporary version of Thomism this is expressed in the idea of human fulfilment, which is the achievement of irreducible basic goods that correspond to the natural goals of human effort.[7]

IV. Aquinas and Kant

The approach that relies on a transcendental interpretation of Aquinas' natural-law theory in the light of Kant's critical moral theory is based on two presuppositions. First, it recognizes the independence of practical reason, which, unlike speculative reason, has its own principles and modes of judgment that are not deducible from the speculative form. Moral values and practical goods are not primarily recognized by the theoretical reason speculatively or empirically, only then, secondarily, to be 'applied' or 'transposed' like technical knowledge by the practical reason. Instead, the practical reason apprehends moral values and fundamental goods on the basis of its inherent cognitive logic, which differs specifically from that of a theoretical-speculative metaphysics and the natural-scientific and empirical procedure proper to the sciences.

The second instance of a transcendental re-reading of Aquinas' natural-law theory in the light of Kant's moral theory is based on consideration of humans as acting subjects. It inquires into the ineluctable conditions that must be satisfied if free human action is accepted as the form proper to an individually responsible moral subject. This treatment of the theme from the viewpoint of the individual's capability of moral behaviour is in line with Aquinas' own approach in the Prologue to the second main section of the *Summa Theologiae*, which is devoted to the development of ethics. Here humans are portrayed as worthy of consideration as images of God to the extent that they originate their own actions; in other words, insofar as they can exercise their will freely and can control their own actions.[8]

Both the emphasis on the independence of practical reason and the approach from the viewpoint of human moral freedom and the capability of moral action refer to certain aspects of Aquinas' ethics. They invite a transcendental interpretation and a search for the uncircumventable prerequisites that will enable human beings to achieve the fulfilment appropriate to their innermost being by engaging in individually responsible action. In short: Aquinas' natural-law ethics in the light of Kant is a quest for the ineluctable conditions that make free moral action possible. Since human beings are not purely rational creatures, but have to exercise their determination as rational existents while remaining subject to the conditions set by a corporeally bound form of existence, the fundamental goods that condition their moral freedom belong both to the sphere of spiritual and intellectual, and to that of physical life. First of all, they embrace physical life as the basic good pure and simple that also supports a person's spiritual and intellectual actions and makes possible the freedom from compulsion, repression, and constraint that is an indispensable precondition of striving for truth. Kant brings both prerequisites for the capability of moral action – the defence of the physical goods of the human person and the recognition of their rights to freedom – together in the concept of human dignity. This central term has an actual point of connection with Aquinas' ethics, although it does not occupy the dominant position in the Thomist system that it has in Kant's.

V. Fundamental goods and moral values

Both the foregoing assumptions made by a transcendental re-reading of the natural-law theory of Aquinas appear to be acceptably grounded from the viewpoint of contemporary philosophy. They also feature significant differences both from a purely empirico-pragmatic conception of ethics and from an attempt to establish morality comprehensively on the basis of the specific sources of knowledge proper to the Christian faith (biblical revelation, tradition, and the magisterium of the Church). The purely natural-scientific world-view of the modern sciences favours detached observers who stand dispassionately over against the objects which they are examining. The claim advanced by scientific methodology calls for the observers themselves and their faculty of perception to be withdrawn from the objects under observation. To this 'view from nowhere' (Thomas Nagel) the world appears as a *tabula rasa*, a blank screen on which human subjectivity projects its attitudes.[9]

On this basis, the empirical observation of sheer facts (*facta bruta*) does not lead to the knowledge of objective moral values or of practical goods that are fundamental and normatively significant. Yet a genuinely practical relation to the world is not possible from a purely observational perspective. It is made available only by participating in a common existential practice, whose necessary implications may conceal patterns of transcendental argument in ethics. From this participational viewpoint, practical values and natural human goals – or moral values (to use a term that is popular outside the academic discussion of ethics) – appear as components of the common world. They are grasped as such by the practical reason, which provides the motivation for their realization without needing to explain them away as dubious ontological entities somewhat akin to the Platonic ideas.

Moral goods or values are actually objects of human aspiration recognized by practical reason, and belong to that specific area of reality which is the sphere of common moral activity. Just as forms of human activity include

practice as a prime mode of communicative action alongside purely technical production, the topography of ontology comprises not only the world
of natural things and objective products but the sphere of practical goods
to whose accomplishment human activity is directed. The practical ethical
relation to the world disclosed in communicative activity presupposes a
more comprehensive ontology than that available in the scientific view of
the world.[10]

Practical values and truly worthwhile goals in life are natural to humans,
and are arrived at by a specific kind of knowledge proper to practical reason.
Although a natural-law theory derived from Aquinas and Kant would rely on
the difference between practical judgments regarding our action in the world
and empirical knowledge of the world, this does not reduce the effectiveness of the empirical approach, for no one could deny that a scientific outlook is appropriate to our understanding of the world in the modern era.
Nevertheless, a rigidly scientific type of reasoning does reach the bounds of
its possibilities when it comes to the knowledge of good and evil and to evalu-
ating moral suasions. Any attempts to answer questions about the practical
conduct of life by referring to empirical methods of apprehending nature are
necessarily based on illogical reasoning and must culminate in a fundamental
categorical error. This confusion of two spheres of reality and of two types of
reasoning is surely due to the essentially erroneous character of a naturalistic
world view, and what might justly be called the naturalistic fallacy.

VI. Basic conditions of a specifically human existence

The second presumption of a transcendental natural-law theory derived
from Aquinas and Kant (an approach involving the human capacity for
moral behaviour that is the normative essence of the dignity proper to every
single human being) requires its demarcation from the kind of essential-
ist and a-historical approach to natural law that necessarily derives binding
conclusions not only about the ways in which individuals shape their lives,
but about the social order, from a static conception of human nature.

The idea of human dignity tends to be interpreted instead in the sense
of a minimal concept that covers no more than the indispensable prerequisites of a specifically human mode of existence. It evokes the initial conditions which afford human beings a life requiring them to exercise their own
rationally guided responsibility by untrammelled striving to achieve basic
practical goods (life, friendship, sex, procreation, play, creativity, scientific
knowledge, and the pursuit of truth), in which they can fulfil their existence.

Nevertheless, a transcendental interpretation of natural law does not offer a comprehensive concept of the good life but makes room for more discriminating and far-reaching anthropological constructions of the kind already made available for a Christian ethics by the scriptural image of humanity and its interpretation of fundamental human experiences (gender, sexuality, health, sickness, the communal life of rich and poor, interacting with strangers and foreigners, our attitude to power and possession, and so on).

Translated by J.G.Cumming

Notes

1. See especially Seneca's ninetieth letter: Seneca, *Ad Lucilium epistolae morales*, 90.4; 90.44ff; also Felix Flückiger, *Geschichte des Naturrechts*, Vol. I: *Altertum und Frühmittelalter*, Zürich, 1954, pp. 215–8.
2. Cf. Ernst Bloch, *Naturrecht und menschliche Würde*, Frankfurt am Main, 1977, pp. 76–9.
3. See in this respect Pierre Hadot, *Exercices spirituels et philosophie antique*, Paris, 1981.
4. *Summa theologiae* I-II, 18.5 (*The Summa Theologica of St Thomas Aquinas*, vol. I, New York, 1947, pp. 665–6).
5. Cf. *De Veritate* 21.1 and the commentary: A. J. Lisska, *Aquinas' Theory of Natural Law. An Analytic Reconstruction*, Oxford, 1996, pp. 182–9.
6. Cf. *Summa theologiae* I-II, 94.2 and ad 2 (*op. cit.*, p. 1009).
7. On the criticism of the neo-Scholastic understanding of *lex naturalis* see M. Rhonheimer, *Natur als Grundlage der Moral. Eine Auseinandersetzung autonomer und theologischer Ethik*, Innsbruck & Vienna, 1985, pp. 36–42; on the dynamic thrust of Aquinas' ethics see H. B. Veatch, 'Natural is-ought-question', in: *id.*, *Swimming against the Current in Contemporary Philosophy. Occasional Essays and Papers*, Washington, 1990, 293-311, esp. 302ff; R. A. Gauthier, *La morale d'Aristote*, Paris, 1958, pp. 47f. and A. J. Lisska, *op. cit. supra*, 196ff.
8. Cf. *Summa theologiae* I-II, Prologue and I 21.1 ad 2.
9. See: J. H. McDowell, *Mind, Value and Reality*, Cambridge, Mass., 1998, pp.39ff.
10. *Ibid.*, pp. 70 and 139ff.

Natural Law and Bioethics

LUDWIG SIEP

Questions of traditional and modern natural law are raised in different ways in contemporary debates about bioethics.[1] On the one hand, we are faced with far-reaching modifications of 'nature': of, that is, the characteristics and processes of the sentient and especially the non-sentient world, including the constitution of the human body and the reproduction of the species, that until now have remained independent of human volition. Consequently we have to ask whether we are concerned here with arbitrarily accessible material, or with qualities and structures of value subject to moral and legal considerations. On the other hand, the question of what is 'naturally right' is posed in an age of growing availability of technology and of democratic standardization. Are there such things as norms that exist outside the variable arrangements of democratic majorities, or irrespective of tribunals subject to the influence of judicial appointments and the 'dominant concepts of law'? In fact there are notions of natural law, especially those refined in the modern European era, that do not acknowledge the idea of an external, purposive, and 'action-orientated' nature to which values can be ascribed, and that subscribe instead to the essentiality (the 'nature') of human reason. These concepts of natural law have indeed held on to such immutable standards.

Today, too, a form of natural law in both acceptations is to be found mainly in Christian traditions – in Catholic natural law or in the Protestant ethos of creation ('preserving creation'). In these cases even apparently 'orthodox' viewpoints, which are often portrayed as unchanging projections of pre-modern metaphysics, react emphatically to changes in the scientific view of the world (in, say, the theory of evolution) and in historical awareness (changing values). In his 2005 volume of collected addresses *Werte in Zeiten des Umbruchs* (Values in Times of Upheaval), the present Pope (then Cardinal Joseph Ratzinger) asserted that, 'Simplifying the situation somewhat, one might say that we are faced with two fundamental contrary viewpoints, which occur in different versions, and clash to a certain extent. On the one hand, we have the radical relativist position that would exclude the

44

concept of the good (and thereby of truth) from politics entirely, because it is a threat to freedom. "Natural law" is rejected on suspicion of metaphysics, in order to profess relativism consistently. Then there would be no political principle apart from the majority decision' (pp. 5ff).[2] The present Pope names Richard Rorty and Hans Kelsen as philosophical and jurisprudential representatives of this relativism. The danger of this position is said to be that 'the majority are elevated to the status of something like a divinity' against which 'no appeal is then possible' (p. 58). On the other hand, he says, we have natural law, which holds that there are absolute moral and legal truths that are rationally discernible and antedate democracy. Ratzinger cites first Plato and then the Thomist philosopher Jacques Maritain as representatives of the natural-law viewpoint but objects to the Platonic assumption of a timeless reason: 'In practice, however, there is no pure rational evidence independent of history' (p. 63). He classifies the history of revelation and religion in particular as history, which means that Christianity would then be characterized not only by its higher or more authentic revelation but especially by its 'openness to reason'. This faculty has enabled it to enjoy experiences that, like the necessary separation of State and religion, and disclaiming the political and violent imposition of religious truths, are to some extent still impending for other religions.

Nevertheless, in another paper reproduced in the same volume, Ratzinger is sceptical about natural law: 'The concept of natural law presupposes a conception of nature in which nature and reason cooperate and nature itself is rational. This view of nature came to naught with the theory of evolution. . . . Human rights have survived as the last element of natural law, intended in essence to be a law of reason, at least in modern times' (pp. 35ff.). But human rights would have to be supplemented with a theory of 'human duties' and by asking 'whether there might not be a natural reason and consequently a rational law for humans and their stance in the world. A debate of this kind would have to be expounded and applied interculturally' (p. 36).

I suspect that the Pope sees most modern bioethics as an expression of democratic relativism. In fact, a great number of views somewhat unconditionally fall in with changing human desires. Approaches of this kind consider ethics and law on the basis of maximizing the fulfilment of individual preferences, or of a modifiable contract that would ensure the satisfaction of the greatest possible number of individual wishes and the disappointment of the least possible number. The supreme yardstick of achievement combines the autonomy of individual interests and the avoidance of damage for those concerned. For such viewpoints there is no such thing as a nature that would preordain its own measures of actions or would possess a range of values that humans might fulfil or dispense with. This is also true of the physical nature of human beings, which can be subject just as much as external nature to desires for self-improvement or even 'transhumanist' enhancement.

It seems blatantly obvious that we cannot simply contrast a form of natural law, derived from a timeless reason in the Platonic sense, with an individualism of the foregoing kind. Even the Pope admits that there could also be 'alternative positions' between the two alternatives, which he himself represents as 'simplifying' the situation. In fact he cites Karl Popper's conception in this respect. My concern in the following pages is to see whether it is possible to elaborate a position that takes account of experience with natural law *and* the autonomy of the individual in the technological era but does so in a way different to those of currently dominant viewpoints. I think it is possible to take into account the growth of technological freedom of action, the liberation of the individual from superfluous suffering, and historical experiences with values and standards, and yet to avoid completely instrumentalizing nature and entirely relativizing norms. There are four stages in my argument. In the first stage (I), I examine three fundamental aspects of traditional natural law; in the second (II), I cite some major aspects of the transformation of these notions in modern times; in the third (III), I offer a summary account of the relationship between the inheritance of nature and latitude of action in the type of ethics which I have in mind; and, in the final stage (IV), I describe some consequences for practical themes in bioethics.

I. Three fundamental aspects of traditional natural law

When referring to natural law in the following pages, I am concerned not so much with the Platonic as with the Aristotelian tradition and its transformation in the modern period. For want of the necessary competence, I shall refer only quite peripherally to medieval forms of natural law. From now on, moreover, I am interested not in proffering the precise analyses proper to a historian of philosophy, but in characterizing a type and tradition of thinking about ethics and the philosophy of right (law).

It is certainly a matter for debate whether we may justly apply the term 'natural law' to the traditional basis of ethics and politics established by the Greeks. Nevertheless, Plato, Aristotle, and the Stoa were convinced that there was something *physei dikaion*: that which is right according to nature, and by which positive laws and morals could be assessed. It was also commonly held that the just or right could be found both in the elucidation of external nature and by reflecting on the constitution of the human soul and the social order appropriate to its capabilities. Any such order must be especially appropriate to the rational nature of the human being. For all three schools of philosophy, the natural order was teleological. In other words, given favourable conditions and careful inner control and direction, natural, spiritual (intellectual), and social processes could reach a state of maturity experienced from without as prospering and 'flourishing', and from within as fulfilment, or *eudaimonia*.

This teleological constitution of natural, intellectual and social processes comprises the first of the three fundamental aspects of this conception, which have exerted an essential influence on the entire development of natural law. The second aspect, which was especially evident in the case of Aristotle, consists in the view of human life in the civic community of the *polis* (the city in the sense of Aristotle's *Politics*) as determinative. The third aspect, which the abovementioned schools of thought share, if with certain differences of emphasis, consists in the inner reason of humans, their reflective or conscientious insight, which provides them with behavioural guidelines which they find personally persuasive and generally valid.

I shall examine these three aspects in more detail, for from the start they contained a certain tension that became more acute in the modern era.

(1) Without discussing the type and extent of the Aristotelian teleology of nature in fine detail, it is important to note that Aristotle sees living creatures at least as possessing what might be called inner programmes that control the process by which they grow and mature, and which enable them to carry out their species-specific functions. Sentient creatures always find it pleasurable to live in a way appropriate to their species. It is necessary to deal with other creatures appropriately in order to assist their due development. In any case, the aims of all higher forms of life can intervene in the determinative aspects of lower forms of life and use them for their own purposes. Accordingly, Aristotle talks of the *ergon*, the specific form of life and performance of a horse or a beast of burden, as if it were something self-evident. But Aristotle would not have considered a horse to be a good mount if it had not been properly bred and nurtured from an early age, all the way to pinpointed muscle development. Moreover, human beings rely on certain potentials in the nature of a creature which they can utilize for their own purposes if they develop them in a certain direction. Even then, a stud-horse must still duly express its species-specific mode of being or it will be of no use to its owner. As we know, Aristotle also saw the relationship between master and slave

(that is, between a master and a living creature merely capable of obeying rational instructions) as a mutually advantageous symbiosis of this kind.

A recasting of lower by higher goals is also found in processes of natural growth. Similarly, with regard to the development of the human embryo, Aristotle proceeds from a kind of graduation of the formal and purposive elements of the soul from the vegetable through the animal to the human soul proper, which then begins to control human development only after some considerable time has elapsed. As we know, Thomas Aquinas held that this notion of gradual ensoulment was compatible with biblical teaching.[3]

I need only mention the fact that, with the doctrine of creation, Christian natural law attributed another supernatural origin to Aristotle's immanent teleology, which was sustained by the 'loving attraction' of a self-conceiving unmoved mover. This modification did little to change the exemplariness and worthiness of imitation of natural purposive processes. It was not until the voluntarism of the late Middle Ages (if Hans Blumenberg is right[4]) that ideas of the Creator and their expression in terms of natural law were succeeded by God's infinite creative power as worthy of imitation, with consequences for the ideal of creativity and innovation that we find so riveting only now in the technological era. I shall return to this point later (cf. II below).

(2) The second distinctive feature of natural law, especially in the Aristotelian acceptation, is that each human by nature or essence is *zoon politikon*, a being intended to live in the *polis*.[5] The extent to which the small Greek State ruled by a securely established city as its 'core territory' can be compared with the present-day concept of State and politics need not concern us here. The essential thing is the tension in this very idea of the *zoon (physei) politikon*. It means, first, that specifically human powers can develop purposively only in a particular form of community, and that the political commonwealth can emerge as the ultimate form of fulfilment as the result of a natural purposive process of community formation beyond house and village – though of course only if no disturbances or mistakes intervene to prevent this.

Second, the essential element of human political expression and reason is publicly conducted debate, especially before a public assembly and court, on questions of justice and injustice, of utility or potential harm.[6] This debate was decided by means of different procedures, including majority votes. Aristotle was not unaware of the fact that the debate about justice had an open historical dimension. In the *Ethics* he issued a challenge to the idea of an ultimate legal statute in matters of norms and standards. According to him, it was much more a matter of prudent decision-making appropriate to the situation and to those concerned, after mature consideration and on the basis of specific fundamental rational-emotional attitudes – the virtues. And in politics it was a question of adaptation to the particular varying circumstances of location, climate, the principal means of employment, changing situations among nations, and so on. Consequently, different constitutions could be appropriate to human nature, and what was essentially right could take different legal forms. Not only democracy, but all polities that promoted the common good could be good and just as far as Aristotle was concerned.

In other words, the naturally rational and therefore political creature also had to discover what was right and good by engaging in processes of consultation and decision about changing situations and customs. Therefore people could not simply 'imitate' a preordained outer or inner nature but had to find out what was appropriate to human beings even under changing circumstances.

(3) Consideration of the third aspect of traditional natural law reveals a keener tension between a preordained order and open seeking for what is right. The Socratic discovery of the inner voice, which later becomes the concept of the self-examining conscience, contributes to the idea of what was naturally right and good an individual instance of possible deviation from preordained arrangements (even, in certain circumstances, to the point of tragic or revolutionary conflict). This inner reflection had two aspects from the start. On the one hand, it subjected the existing order, and everything that common sense pronounced to be moral, to the criterion of individual performability. On the other hand, it brought one's own interests, wishes, and opinions before the judgment of a reason that was equally subject to all rational beings.

In the modern period this led to the development of a rational law that no longer seeks the right in imitation of the natural order or the changing morality of the *polis*, but looks for it primarily in reason, which is accessible by means of reflection and subjective thinking. This leads to the possibility of conflicts between the rational laws of the general will and the protest of the individual conscience, which Hegel, for instance, discusses so exhaustively in the *Phenomenology* and the *Philosophy of Right* – although his solution of the problem is somewhat 'Hellenist'.[7]

It would be inappropriate to discuss the variable ranking of the three abovementioned elements of traditional natural law any further here. Nevertheless, we may concede that the role of conscience is more significant in the Socratic-Stoic tradition than in Aristotle – although there is also a form of inward reflection in Aristotle with aspects both of universality and rule-following and of reference to the person and to the situation.[8]

In traditional natural law, natural teleology, political prudence with reference to a specific community and its experiences, and general reason accessible in inner reflection and scrutiny of conscience formed a unity which certainly had its tensions yet could be brought to the point of equilibrium. It came increasingly under pressure as natural law developed in the modern era, from the sixteenth to the nineteenth century. This pressure was exerted mainly from three directions: First, the teleological explanation of nature yielded to the mechanico-technological theory of development, and finally to the theory of evolution as subject to chance. Second, the limits were partly removed from processes of historical experience. Third, the autonomy of the individual ran counter to every kind of predetermined natural or legal and rational order.

II. Some major aspects of transformation

In 1821 Hegel published the first edition of his (Berlin) *Grundlinien der Philosophie des Rechts* (Elements of the Philosophy of Right) and appended the subtitle *Naturrecht und Staatswissenschaft im Grundrisse* (Natural Law and Political Science in Outline). For Hegel natural law was still a vital concept, although he had already dismissed some of the traditional assumptions associated with it. He saw external nature as devoid of any inherent right or normative structure pre-given to the rational will. Like Kant, he thought that the principles of relations between persons and things, and between persons and other persons, were provided by an order immanent to the rational will ('A person must translate his freedom into an external sphere in order to exist as Idea. . . . What is immediately different from free mind is that which, both for mind and in itself, is the external pure and simple, a thing, something not free, not personal, without rights. . . . It is my mind which of all things I can make most completely my own. . . . In face of the free will, the thing retains no property in itself, even though there still remains in possession . . . something external').[9] The determinative constitution of nature was to be appropriated by human beings, and to make possible higher purposive determinations of the spirit (mind). Therefore natural law was to be understood as rational law. Yet reason was not a timeless structure of Platonic ideas but developed and came to understand itself in an historical learning process. This process was directed to growth in awareness and institutions of freedom, of individuals, and of nations.

Although such modifications of natural law are to be found in Hegel, his philosophy as a whole still has a 'traditionalist' inclination, and he still attributes goal-directed processes orientated to equilibrium to certain areas of nature, which is a conception very distant from the ideas of the mechanists.[10] Since Hobbes, they had absolutely rejected any explanation of natural processes that postulated a dependence on immanently purposive attributes. To explain living creatures and natural processes one had only to search for effective causes, and then to understand them by at least theoretically dismantling all structures and reducing them to the smallest possible fragments before reconstructing them. This association of technical reproducibility (and later of perfectibility) and biological enlightenment has lasted down to our own times, although the extreme mechanistic approach of the seventeenth to nineteenth centuries has now been superseded.

The modern explanation of nature is very dependent on the extended possibilities of human action and of the use of nature. This dependence was also evident in certain philosophers, such as John Locke, who continued to support a natural law partly deducible from the form and uninterrupted development of living creatures. Locke's system proposed a counterbalance between, on the one hand, a natural law dependent on the will of God, and, on the other hand, individual autonomy and experimental and technical mastery of nature.[11] The main reason for his attachment to natural law was experience of the arbitrary nature of the absolute monarch superior to all laws. Locke proposed instead a distribution of the functions of power and adoption of the majority principle in the legislative body. Nevertheless, he was reluctant to place all moral and legal boundaries at the disposition of this majority, for then, he maintained, the majority would meet with the same violent opposition on the basis of conscience offended by the violation of fundamental rights that had been evoked by the absolute ruler.

Nevertheless, Locke and the Royal Society (one of the nuclei of modern science and technology) abandoned the notion of a purposively and necessarily ordered nature. The divine 'determination' of nature did not reside in its immanently purposive development but in its immaturity and improvability. It indicated the scope of the task faced by the human race in seeking to complete an unfinished creation. Experience and technological interventions – Locke, for instance, supervised the first operation on the liver, carried out to remove a hydatid cyst from the Earl of Shaftesbury – revealed both the regularity of natural processes and the ways in which they can help to raise human living standards. Furthermore, human social life should be regulated not by innate moral rules, but with the aid of reflection on cultural experiences, where chance events – such as the introduction of the monetary system – play a significant role.

Locke's view of natural law as compatible with the experiential sciences, the technical instrumentalization of nature and the autonomy of the individual depended on his concept of experience, which was extremely influential in the modern era. Methodically informed experiential knowledge is the source of all awareness of natural and moral laws. But these experiences make us conscious of a particular minimally conflictual arrangement of human wishes. Initially, the only one of three abovementioned aspects of natural law to be discarded was the teleology of external nature; and accordingly, in Locke, the notions of substance and species as well as their fixed boundaries. For Locke, therefore, even biological adherence to the human species was not unequivocally knowable. In his system, accordingly, the concept of the person, with an emphasis on memory and imputability in morals and law, replaced the concept of the human being – with consequences extending into modern Anglo-American bioethics. Locke also recognized the notion of a developing person, as is evident in his developed right of children.

Of course, natural law was discredited not only because of its minimal theoretical explanatory value compared with the modern search for an investigation of natural causal processes on the basis of preceding effective causes and conditional events, but because legitimizing a hierarchical social order by appealing to its supposed teleological natural order and to a hierarchy of living things was already obsolescent. The Protestant revolution of conscience, the achievement of religious freedom and of property and contractual freedom, and other fundamental rights, gradually reduced the importance of this social order based on purpose and rank, at least in normative theory. Then the subsequent decisive contribution to the emancipation of the individual made by the technological activity of middle-class proprietors and entrepreneurs has been a theoretical commonplace since Locke, Hegel, and Marx. Above all, the historicization of nature and of normative awareness in the nineteenth century helped to discredit natural law after the 'bourgeois revolutions' had started to dislodge it.

The present Pope does not contest the fact that the theory of evolution has deprived the idea of an ultimately purposively and exemplarily ordered nature of any power to convince, but he would be much more radically opposed to the modifications of value and multiplicity of values arising from historical awareness, and from the development of ethnology and historical scholarship applied to cultural development.

An essential element of traditional natural law may be the notion of an unchangeable, purposive order of external nature and human action accessible to reason, but since the nineteenth century the theory of evolution and historical awareness have called both components in question: the purposive and necessary order of sensually experienced nature and the non-experiential character of normative reason, or reason that acknowledges the existence of standards. The former was replaced by a process in which cosmic and historical geopolitical processes as well as the mutations and mixtures of genetic material contain an ineluctable factor of chance. This also affects the biological species and their reproduction.

But the second aspect or form of natural law, the postulate of a supra-positive reason independent of experience as the source of standardization or the recognition of norms, is directly concerned here. Admittedly, in the modern era natural law in the sense of rational law[12] has sought increasingly to liberate itself from the notion of the exemplariness or significant value of nature (I shall return later to the question whether in so doing it has not also disposed of the measures of 'biotechnical' action). But it has held on to the concept of timeless rational norms. This position has been questioned by historical awareness and historical research since the nineteenth century. Today it is possible to identify, say, the 'communitarian ethics of solidarity of free peasants' as the cultural-historical background of the Ten Commandments.[13] Of course this does not mean that the significance of the Commandments and their binding nature depend entirely on such presuppositions. But the time-bound and culture-bound nature of many notions of value has become increasingly clear. Nowadays, for instance, we find it very difficult to understand the scruples which prevented some of those plotting to kill Hitler from breaking their oath of obedience to their 'Leader'.

III. Consequences for practical themes in bioethics

Instead of pursuing this development any further, I must now ask where it has been taken in contemporary philosophical ethics, and especially bioethics.

In order to emphasize the basic options, I shall simplify the following remarks to a certain extent. It is evident that a considerable number of modern moralists think of the reality of nature as what is revealed by the natural sciences. This nature, as for Locke, features causal processes and the degree to which they can be influenced. The association of technology and enlightenment has become much closer in modern science. This applies not only to scientific modes of procedure, which depend extensively on the technical devices used for observation and measurement, and to a considerable extent on the modification of natural processes. In modern biology, biotechnology alone has opened up new research possibilities. It also applies to the aims of science, which are increasingly orientated to the wishes of society. But they in their turn accord with the means that condition the fulfilment of most private wishes: health, the provision of opportunities for acquisition, and the availability of technologies of communication and movement.

These goals are the result of an at least conjectured agreement of individual wishes. Valuations originate with these wishes and not with any nature or 'fact as such'. Nature is held to be entirely value-free. It is, to use Max Weber's now cliché-like term, 'disenchanted'.[14] It is then left to ethics and law to discover and to justify the rules that allow the greatest possible number of private wishes to be satisfied and the least possible number to be frustrated. This includes many desires for physical improvement of the human body, both one's own and the bodies of one's progeny. If, apart from the universal conditions of equality before the law and self-determination, no further norms can be indicated as applicable to these wishes, the estimates of technological modification of the human body must eventually be left to the majority decisions of democratic voting or the demand for 'marketable' offers of enhancement.

On the other hand, we may try more or less to keep to natural law – either the traditional natural law, or the variety that is orientated to the teleology of natural efforts and developments, or at least to a form that is reduced to human rights, as cited by Joseph Ratzinger. As he indicated, it is also possible to try to draw on the religious traditions of various cultures, in order to interpret the human location in nature by recourse to a viewpoint other than the scientific. But then we have to ask how far this is compatible with scientifically well-founded theories such as the theory of evolution. It is also necessary to avoid re-furnishing any such normative theories with biological pronouncements. Nevertheless, in terms of biological science a fertilized ovum of any species does not possess the determination or *telos* that will enable it to develop into a complete living creature. Biologically, it merely contains the potential to do so under certain specific conditions. In the case of human beings, to do so certain treatments are necessary if fertilization takes place outside the body. Human technological possibilities are making it increasingly feasible to provide this potential by means of biotechnical procedures, as is shown by recent successes in reprogramming differentiated cells.

Moreover, natural law as rational law – that is, existing independently of a purposive nature or a nature of values – is another theoretical option. But a dilemma is discernible here too. Either rational law is understood substantially – as when, for example, we need to assert that specific commandments, such as the Ten Commandments, say, or rights such as human rights, are deducible from a pure reason accessible to all human beings at all times (and I am just as sceptical as Cardinal Ratzinger about such a reason outside history as the source of specific norms) – or reason is understood as a procedure, and accordingly, especially in ethics, as with a contract or discourse. But procedures of this kind do not give rise to a practical content without certain presuppositions. Either they resort, as with John Rawls, to a political culture, that is, to a social democracy based on fundamental rights, which they reconstruct on the basis of favourable considered justifications.[15] Or they take the wishes and the normative proposals of participants as a starting-point, as in discursive ethics. But then, once again, we are faced with the problem of either justifying only standards that will avoid conflicting wishes, or of resorting to common concepts of value associated with particular traditions. In my view, the very procedures themselves are based on historically 'acquired' values such as equality, individual autonomy, fairness, and so forth.[16]

Before discussing the question of a third possibility, I shall give a summary account of the modern situation with regard to the three principles of traditional natural law.

(1) The teleological conception of nature has been abandoned as a scientific explanation in the sense of purposive causation, on the physical and biochemical levels at least. Furthermore, in developmental biology, and in certain areas of behavioural biology, goal-directed modes of behaviour have been as it were reconstructed on the basis of genetic causation.[17] Admittedly, natural self-regulation processes in, say, the areas of self-preservation, growth, and health may feature immanent standard or projected conditions. But a cybernetic or teleonomic explanation does not start by determining natural processes and movements in order to reach its 'natural' goals.

There has been a qualitative change in the use of natural processes for human ends. Even in the time of Aristotle these were not self-contained processes but were already available to be used for the benefit of human ends and practical applications. In the early modern period there was a shift in the ratio in favour of the further technical development of a nature which was thought to be unfinished. In the modern era there has been a dramatic growth of technical capacities for controlling and modifying natural processes in order to reduce hardship, liberate people from suffering, and extend the spheres of possible intervention and experience. In medicine possibilities of technological modification are now becoming available to deal with natural problems that were not considered to be illnesses or diseases in the traditional sense, such as infertility, birth risks and the burdens imposed by genetically impaired children, and by aging and degenerative processes, and so forth. The legitimacy of using medical means to combat these scourges is central to the contemporary debate about medical ethics.

(2) Naturally political human beings have been depoliticized in very many respects in modern society, and are now more likely to see themselves only as individuals holding rights to enjoy specific freedoms and goods. Although no one would deny anyone's right to political cooperation in a modern democracy, few people exercise that right beyond going to vote. Just think of the extent to which people's relation to the State has been transformed from a political to a technical affair.[18] People expect State services to provide technical benefits, and 'administrative' and 'management' staff are expected to dole these things out. Nevertheless, experiences of state control by technocratic elites show that ultimately, even in modern 'public-service societies', people refuse to be permanently deprived of their right to a say in political matters. Our awareness of freedom (as Hegel reminds us) is not so easily forgotten.

So many different ways of looking at the world also make it difficult to obtain a rational consensus with regard to what is just or unjust, useful or destructive. One of the causes of this pluralism is the third aspect, the emancipation of the individual conscience, or the right to change one's community of belief or world-view as one's personal convictions dictate, but also to express one's religious beliefs actively and openly. Other causes are increased mobility and unforced migration. Under such conditions, the common basis for public moral and legal decisions consists essentially of (what Rawls terms) an 'overlapping consensus' about fundamental rights and constitutional principles. It is 'overlapping' because everyone can offer a different justification for it drawn from his or her own world view.[19] But this opportunity to express one's own reasons for holding an opinion must be freely available to all. It is not permissible to maintain, for instance, that atheists might well pay lip-service to the principles of human dignity and human rights but could never justify them.[20] Those unable to justify their actions will scarcely be taken seriously as rational fellow-citizens.

(3) The third principle of traditional natural law, which is the judgment of positive standards by measuring them against the general yardsticks of

the individual conscience, is certainly maintained in the normative order of modern democracies. The rights of refusal for reasons of conscience are stronger in most civilized modern States where the rule of law obtains. In German basic or constitutional law, the right of resistance has been adopted from the English and associated legal traditions, and opportunities to test positive laws in accordance with basic rights are guaranteed.

Nevertheless, it is questionable how far the claim of rational universality goes, and how it is supported. The concept of a non-experiential and a-historical reason is problematical, which means that we have to realize the rational, meaning universally applicable and convincing, consequences of our experience of norms, laws, constitutions, and orders of rule. Moreover, a common cultural memory must have been retained of the kind that emerged in Europe, especially from experiences of religious civil wars, absolutism, industrialization, and the varieties of twentieth-century totalitarianism. It is worth asking whether a hypothetical divine moral standpoint, which can also modify our absolute view of persons and their interests as against nature as a whole, is not still possible and might prove fruitful precisely in bioethics. I shall return to this point when concluding this article.

First, however, it is important to realize that the abandonment of an unrelentingly metaphysical teleology, and of course of its application to the social hierarchy, has contributed to the freedom of the individual in the same way as the technical facilitation of food production, the medical combating of diseases, and the extension of the average lifespan. The use made by individuals and by society of technical means to achieve these desirable ends is an undeniable boon and to a considerable degree both a right of the individual and a duty of the State. But it is questionable in modern bioethics whether, and where, limits should be set to this technical mastery of nature. In a modern democracy it is obvious *who* should decree those limits with binding legislative power: the legislature. But the legislative authority has set limits to its own power in order to avoid 'democratic totalitarianism', for instance, as far as human dignity and the essential content of basic rights are concerned. Of course the 'political body' is entitled to a say in their interpretation and consequences, and religious communities and philosophical and ethical systems can also take part in this dialogue.

Has natural law still any part to play in this debate? The answer to this question has to be defined in accordance with both aspects of the concept of 'natural law'. First, to what extent can natural orders or processes still direct human actions? Second, can timeless standards still exist independently of opinions and subjective desires? To be sure, as modern natural law or the law of reason shows, the two aspects can be separated. It is possible to posit a timeless legal basis even without the guidance of (outer and inner) nature. For modern bioethics, however, it is especially important to ask whether and to what extent it is still permissible to speak of evaluative and normative aspects of nature. In view of this, I shall return to both kinds of natural law and try to give a general answer to my question before discussing more practical bioethical consequences.

(a) I think that the question of a transformation of the heritage of natural law with regard to the structures of inner and outer nature is whether a technological approach to nature can still take the form of (to put it metaphorically) a dialogue, or whether a complete reduction of nature to the condition of material for satisfying arbitrary human desires is the only way that agrees with human autonomy and interests. How are human purposes to treat the potential capacities of natural processes and objects? Surely the processes of evolution and the constitution of the human body that has developed within them, as well as the process of its natural reproduction, also possess certain values that modern biotechnical medicine ought to take into consideration? And surely biotechnical medicine ought to be particularly concerned to do so when humans quite justifiably invoke its help to counter the negative aspects of disease, deformity, degeneration, and untimely death? But should we expect extra-human nature to respond with as it were streamlined precision to any wishes whatsoever, or do the spontaneous modification of inherited genetic material in species evolution, the assertion of rights over its territory even in the face of human competition, the genetic individualization of living creatures in sexual reproduction, and so on, have a specific value that must be weighed against human interests? If the latter is true, then we might legitimately speak of a persistence of natural law in the modern technological treatment of nature.

(b) With regard to the second aspect of natural law, the perennial validity of standards, we have to ask whether the alternative consists only of an extra-historical applicability on the one hand, and a historical relativism of continually changing values on the other hand. Surely there is another possibility: that of a historically informed reason that restricts to the future its claims to validity in the light of basic norms? It is certainly possible to speak of a general moral standpoint arising in the case of early discoveries of certain standards: the Golden Rule in early Chinese philosophy, the Ten Commandments in Israel, or fundamental institutions of early legal developments (such as the introduction of the impartial third party or referee), or of the '*audiatur et altera pars*' (there is yet another side to be heard to every question).

What religions see as revelations or prophetic visions may also be viewed by religious sceptics as discoveries of values that have contributed to the development of moral and legal culture. Concepts and models of the good or right life can either take precedence as visions and postulates of social reality or depend on deductions from experiences of collective suffering. Here there are analogies to the relation between scientific modelling (or subsequent explanation) and experience that could prompt a non-reductive comparison.

There is, however, no linear development in moral culture. Later experiences may also be seen as restrictions and a radicalization of moral values – as with exaggerations of warlike courage, for instance, or allegiance and loyalty to secular and spiritual authorities. Relaxations of ethical and legal norms – with regard to social hierarchies or relations between the sexes – are undoubtedly associated with reduced stringency. But new ideals of communal life or admirable moral behaviour can also arise in close dependence on external conditions.[21]

It is undeniable that diametrically opposed moral traditions have emerged during the further development of the moral outlook, for instance the early Greek culture of revenge and heroic combat as opposed to the Christian teaching of the Sermon on the Mount. But we can observe the origin of common yardsticks for interpreting and judging collective experiences in major intercultural advances, as represented nowadays by human rights, for example.[22] We may hope that they will spread and become permanently established with the increasing universality of experiences in a globalized and mediatized world.

Insights into the ways in which human capabilities have been repeatedly repressed, or into the now available possibility of a worthwhile life free from the personal or ideological domination on which that repression was based, are now historically irreversible. There are no longer any conceivable grounds for a complete revision of human rights. No one can any longer reasonably assert a right to change these rights in any major respect.

Accordingly, in modern ethics we are still entitled to speak of the heritage of natural law in all three respects: not only in maintaining the political nature of human beings and their freedom of conscience, but with regard to adaptation to structures and potentials of natural processes, and finally in asserting the irreversible validity of fundamental standards – at least for a future in which there is still such a thing as a moral standpoint. Of course this presupposes that we shall still be dealing with a comparable 'human' biological species. If the species were to be profoundly altered by radical enhancement measures, for instance by the arrival of a new sub-species with considerable 'attainments' at certain levels, the ideas of equality and justice that have prevailed hitherto – including presuppositions of 'political' communication about common goods – would collapse altogether.

There are excellent reasons for maintaining that human rights are both indebted to the historical development of rational thought and form part of a natural law. I would say that the contribution to this process of different cultures and ways of thinking – and especially the results of the European Enlightenment – are possibly more significant than the present Pope would seem to suppose, when he prefers to invoke intercultural dialogue as mainly responsible for the other aspect of natural law – the place humankind occupies in nature. However that may be, modern science and technology undoubtedly comprise a major reference-point in that dialogue. It would be difficult to dispute their far-reaching unprejudiced explanation of natural processes, and their contribution to the emancipation of the individual from natural pressures and burdens. The critical questions of modern bioethics are concerned precisely with the extent to which technological liberation from natural restrictions is still compatible not only with the adoption of the values enshrined in certain aspects of nature as experienced to date, but at the same time with certain outcomes of moral and legal learning processes.

IV. Consequences for practical themes in bioethics

Consideration of the major bioethical controversies of recent decades shows that they all involve the tensions present in natural law from the start. It is a matter of the relation between natural structures, technical liberation from natural constraints, individual autonomy and supra-individual reason. The most recent step in technological development, biotechnology, has led to a significant increase in these tensions. For instance, gene technology attempts to protect human nutrition from unforeseeable fluctuations in natural processes, such as failed harvests, insect attacks on plants and fruit, damage incurred during transport, and so on. Of course it also tries to enhance pleasure and to achieve certain aesthetic effects. It is hoped that gene technology can be used in animal breeding to protect the results, and ideally animals of optimum utility for human interests, from the accidental disadvantages of future mutations.

Yet a major risk in this context is not only the danger of scarcely predictable interactions and long-term consequences, but a change in the structure of natural life. Until now, of course, natural life included the spontaneous and chance mixing of genes, changes in the sequence of generations and in populations, and individualization in reproduction. Diversity, individuality, and a species-specific life are not simply value-free characteristics of living nature, but part of our precious natural inheritance. New developments in mimetic technology and in the area of norms for dealing with nature show that taking natural processes and extra-human species and forms of life into account is still thought to be worthwhile as far as technology and mastering nature are concerned. This is also increasingly true of global agreements on sustainability, biodiversity, the heritage of landscapes and natural monuments, and so on. As the rejection of chimera formations and of the abandonment of the gradation and order of beings shows, the 'ladder of nature' or Great Chain of Being (*scala naturae*) is still seen as a valuable natural yardstick for human activity.

The relevant question in natural and environmental ethics is whether it is possible to govern the biotechnical treatment of nature by an accommodation between reducing human suffering and appropriating the natural heritage instead of just following individual desires and satisfying them in processes controlled by market demands and majority opinion. This heritage clearly comprises a many-sided nature that is partly independent of human wishes and a flourishing existence of individualized life forms, each in its own way. Of course, this does not necessarily mean that we have to protect every natural enemy of humankind, including pathogens, or that we must completely abandon the breeding of useful animals, even when using biotechnical methods to do so.

Nevertheless, much more acute tensions in the debate about bioethics have occurred in the area of the technological approach to the human body and its reproduction. Admittedly, nowadays scarcely any ethical viewpoint would still argue that the use of medico-technical means to prevent, combat, or reduce the impact of disease and sickness was unjustifiable. But it is a matter of contention whether there should still be a boundary between, on the one hand, prevention and therapy, and, on the other hand, improvement or optimization actively to hasten the human evolutionary process, as some 'transhumanists' recommend.[23] The extent to which it is permissible to interfere technically in human reproduction is also controversial. Furthermore, since the expectations of modern medicine are heavily invested in the regeneration of organs and tissues from living material, that is, either by transplanting intact organs and tissues or by recourse to self-propagating and self-differentiating cells, ethical problems regarding the use of living human physical material arise in this respect too.

Perhaps the most obvious aspect of influence on human reproduction is the technologization and extension of the possibilities of human activity and experience, and the far-reaching social changes that have resulted from this. For instance, in the age of biochemical contraception, the natural-cum-rational view of the sex drive as directed to reproduction of the human species, and as 'sharing in divine creation' (*participatio creationis divinae*), as found in traditional natural-law theory, to some extent in Aristotle's *oikos* theory, and more explicitly in the Scholastic doctrine of 'natural inclinations' (*inclinationes naturales*), can no longer be taken as universally binding. Physical love has become first and foremost an aspect of sharing, affection, and non-purposive pleasure, and only misanthropes would deny that this change is in any way valuable. Inconsequential sex and effective family planning have also led to vast changes in women's sphere of activity and in relations between the sexes.

Another step in controlling the process of reproduction has been artificial or assisted insemination, which frees people who urgently want children from certain conditions and obstacles associated with natural insemination. These new techniques have also made it possible to distinguish between genetically normal embryos and those in which severe impairments of normal processes or serious diseases are anticipated, so that only those in the first category become actual candidates for birth. Accordingly, it is increasingly possible to replace the natural choice of implantation and pregnancy by a controlled procedure favouring the avoidance of giving birth to a genetically impaired child. It is understandable that mothers would want to take advantage of these possibilities, especially if they run a considerable risk of inheriting major genetic defects.[24] This would seem to be merely another step in the process of liberating women from the possible suffering associated with natural hazards.

But an objection is to be raised here precisely. A technique offering all the foregoing would amount to using the biological potential of the human body merely as material to satisfy arbitrary desires. Highly estimable structures and processes of human nature no longer have to be taken into account, so it seems. But that does not seem to be a necessary conclusion. It is undeniable that many people find severely genetically impaired children a heavy burden, even though those who do decide to tackle the situation often experience great joy or make very praiseworthy sacrifices.[25] Nevertheless, we cannot talk of mere whims being satisfied when people who can be assured of running ever fewer risks associated with natural reproduction refuse to subject themselves to that kind of chance difficulty. I think that this situation must be assessed quite differently from producing the ideal child by methods that might indeed be said to use our natural human potential as material for satisfying arbitrary desires in a much more radical sense.

But surely, from the first moment of the origin of a new individual genome, the human embryo is a human person worthy of human dignity and of the defence of his or her life? Indeed, that is the normative basis of recent German legislation on the protection of embryos. There are certainly good reasons for this, but whether they are compelling is another matter. It is also doubtful whether the legal codes of other countries, which depend on the notion of gradual development to the point of being human and on an increase in worth and rights, are obviously 'barbaric' and naturally and rationally illicit. Such views are much more properly the subject-matter of scientific, but also public political debates and decisions on what is just and unjust, which have been characteristic of human nature since Aristotle.

In my opinion, we are faced here with a question of how we are to draw the boundary between technology and natural structures in a way that contradicts neither autonomy nor moral principles. As I have said, the biological potential of a cell to develop into a complete human being under favourable conditions, which in this case depend on human actions, possesses no normative determination to promote any such process unconditionally. To assert this would either amount to teleology in the pre-modern sense, or would deserve the criticism that this was an illogical naturalist derivation of norms from a fact of biological development.[26] A further argument would maintain that a graduation of dignity and rights to life could eventually cause a breach in the dam, as it were, with regard to the equal rights to protection of all those born human. 'Could eventually . . .' is not really tenable, since breaches in the dam are never more than more or less probable.[27] 'Could eventually cause' is certainly a hypothesis worth considering, especially from a practical legal viewpoint. But it is not evident that another boundary, nidation, say, or implantation, and the corresponding stage of development, might not be standardized and sanctioned as permanent. Norms are always correlated with natural stages of development. Embryos actually have fewer rights than highly-developed foetuses; foetuses fewer than newborn infants; and children fewer than adults.

But surely that means arbitrarily assigning human value and human rights and thus making them dependent on democratic majorities, rather than defining them as a preordained boundary-point for humans and therefore classifying them as withdrawn from arbitrary human decisions and behaviour? But I do *not* think that this is a compelling conclusion either. Both the history of our moral and legal orders and the legislation of a democratic State in which the rule of law prevails can be understood as an attempt to discover what is proper to specific natural structures and stages of development, but above all to human capabilities; to find out, that is, what is normatively appropriate to them. The rights of the human person are preordained, and not the stage of development in which the personality starts or in which subjective rights are granted to the early embryo.

The difficulty we encounter with early human life is also influenced by the fact that, given the constantly-growing possibilities of biotechnology, we have less and less to do with the natural in the sense of objects and processes that might be independent of human volition and action. If progress in influencing the genetic potential of cells continues to advance as it has done hitherto, then it might indeed be possible one day to assign or to restore every potential to each cell.[28] Would we still wish to assert that a body cell that had been rendered 'totipotent' by artificial measures was a person possessed of human dignity, or a new citizen entitled to all rights granted by the State? Or would this development begin only at the point when implantation was made to happen and the path to birth was decided and commenced as a result of conscious explicit activity?

These constellations of technology and natural potentials force us to ask whether another demarcation between human volition, technical possibility, and natural potential would really prepare the way for a wholly arbitrary choice of wishes and their fulfilment. Would an explicit separation of sex, reproduction with possibilities of extended action, and the medical use of totipotent cells *before* implantation, really amount to a crossing of the Rubicon? Or would it remain in the context of a moral standpoint and of dealing with natural potentials which human beings can use to their advantage without reducing them to the level of mere material means of satisfying arbitrary desires?

We shall never finally define the lines of demarcation between nature, technology, and autonomy, for in this respect too we have to remain open to learning processes without surrendering our concern for natural structures and moral principles. Therefore the heritage of natural law ought to remain a vital element of bioethics. In my view, this inherited 'cosmic rationality' should live on, so that we can always adopt a stance of beneficent distance from the specific interests of humankind.[29] A natural-law standpoint of this kind would require human beings to be located in a whole: in, that is, a 'cosmos' in the sense of a conceivable well-intentioned order of nature which not only makes their cultivating and technological action possible but is its necessary field of expression.

Translated by J. G. Cumming

Notes

1 The following text is based on a paper given to the *Haus am Dom* Catholic Academy in Frankfurt am Main in December 2007.

2. Joseph Ratzinger [Pope Benedict XVI], *Werte in Zeiten des Umbruchs. Die Herausforderungen der Zukunft bestehen* (Values in Times of Upheaval), Freiburg im Breisgau, 2005 (subsequent page references are to this edition).

3. In contrast to his teacher Albertus Magnus. Cf. Thomas Aquinas, *Commentarium in Sententiis Magistri Petri Lombardi*, Lib. III, Dist. III, quaest. 5, art. 2, and H. Seidl, 'Zur Geistseele im menschlichen Embryo nach Aristotle, Albertus Magnus und Thomas von Aquin', *Salzburger Jahrbuch für Philosophie*, 1986, pp. 51ff.

4. H. Blumenberg, ,'Nachahmung der Natur', in *idem, Wirklichkeiten, in denen wir leben*, Stuttgart, 1981, pp. 55–103.

5. On the following see Aristotle, *Politics* 1253 a 1–20.

6. Aristotle, *ibid.*, and *Rhetoric* 1358 b.

7. Hegel seeks to renew the Greek 'social order' of the undeniably experienced standards and customs of a politico-religious community on the level of reflection of subjective moral convictions and individual legal freedom. Cf. L. Siep, 'Moralischer und sittlicher Geist in Hegels Phänomenologie', in W. Welsch & K. Vieweg (eds) *200 Jahre Phänomenologie des Geistes*, Frankfurt am Main, 2008 (in press).

8. Cf. Aristotle, *Nicomachean Ethics*, III, 5 and 6.5, 8, and 9. But Aristotle, like the Hellenistic philosophers, still sees no fundamental tension between personal moral insight and political activity.

9. Cf. Hegel, *Grundlinien der Philosophie des Rechts* (*Philosophy of Right*, tr. T. M. Knox, Oxford, 1952), parr. 41, 42, 52.

10. Hegel conceives of them as undeveloped presemblances afforded by the mind (spirit). The mind is therefore the 'pattern' of nature and not the reverse. See in this respect B. Merker, 'Jenseits des Hirns. Zu Hegels Philosophie des subjektiven Geistes', in B. Merker, G. Mohr & M. Quante (eds.), *Subjektivität und Anerkennung*. Paderborn, n.d., pp. 140–66.

11. On natural law in Locke see R. Specht, *John Locke*, Munich, 2007, pp. 148–58. On the following see also L. Siep, *Kommentar zu John Locke, Zweite Abhandlung über die Regierung*, Frankfurt am Main, 2007.

12. At any rate, Kant's rational law proceeds from the assumption that nature

is purposive, as is shown in the way in which he derives the prohibition of suicide.

13. Friedrich Wilhelm Graf, *Moses Vermächtnis. Über göttliche und menschliche Gesetze*. Munich, ²2006, p. 46

14. The imputation of a historical continuity and factual inseparability between magical and all later forms of evaluative concepts of nature is a questionable aspect of this jargon.

15. John Rawls, *A Theory of Justice*, Cambridge, Mass., 1971, ²1999.

16. See in this regard: L. Siep, *Konkrete Ethik*, Frankfurt am Main, 2004, pp. 179ff.

17. Although it is questionable how far we can have recourse to genetics to explain complex modes of behaviour in life forms that are capable of learning.

18. One thinks, for instance, of the writings of Herbert Marcuse and Jürgen Habermas (especially since J. Habermas, 'Technology and Science as "Ideology"', in *Toward a Rational Science*, London, 1971).

19. Cf. John Rawls, 'The Idea of an Overlapping Consensus', in *idem, Political Liberalism*, New York, 1993.

20. See, e.g., R. Spaemann: 'But the idea of human dignity and its inalienability can be grounded only in a metaphysical ontology, i.e. in a philosophy of the absolute. Accordingly atheism deprives the idea of human dignity definitively of any support and therefore of the possibility of theoretical self-assertion in a civilization', 'Über den Begriff der Menschenwürde', in E.-W. Böckenförde &. R. Spaemann (eds), *Menschenrechte und Menschenwürde*, Stuttgart, 1987, pp. 295–316, esp. p. 313.

21. Cf in this respect L. Siep, 'Virtues, Values, and Moral Objectivity', in C. Gill (ed.), *Virtue, Norms, and Objectivity*, Oxford, 2005, pp. 83–98.

22. But also, say, the 'common morality', which is a basic assumption of T. L. Beauchamp and J. F. Childress in their *Principles of Bioethics*, ⁵Oxford, 2001. As an aspect common to most contemporary ethical systems, it would feature the principles of non-maleficience, beneficence (or reciprocal aid), autonomy, and justice.

23. See in this regard L. Siep, 'Die biotechnische Neuerfindung des Menschen', in J. S. Ach & A. Pollmann (eds), *No body is perfect. Baumassnahmen am menschlichen Körper–Bioethische und ästhetische Aufrisse*, Bielefeld (transcript) 2006, pp. 21–42.

24. Particularly if, as in Germany, they are permitted to terminate a developed pregnancy quite legally if they do not find themselves psychologically capable of bearing genetically impaired children to maturity and raising them – a ruling that is problematical in any case in view of the absence of any time limitation.

25. In modern bioethics we also find the view that there is an obligation to prevent the suffering of a severely impaired child. Cf. A. Buchanan, D.W. Brock, N. Daniels, & D. Wikler, *From Chance to Choice*, Cambridge, 2000.

26. Honnefelder tries to go beyond this alternative when, basing himself on Aristotle, he seeks to endow 'human' as a 'sortal predicate' ascribable to 'all individuals of the relevant natural type', with a normatively directed predicate of value associated with the lived world. Cf. L. Honnefelder, 'Bioethik und die Frage nach der Natur des Menschen', in G. Abel (ed.), *Kreativität* (papers given at the 20th German Philosophy Conference, 2005), Hamburg, 2006, pp. 324–38, esp. pp. 330ff.

27. Here I make no distinction between dam-burst and slippery-slope arguments. On the latter, see B. Guckes, *Das Argument der Schiefen Ebene*, Frankfurt am Main, 1997.

28. On the current state of research with reprogrammed cells and the consequences for the concept of totipotency, see: A. Wobus, 'Reversibilität des Entwicklungsstadiums menschlicher Zellen. Stammzellforschung, Potentialitätsprinzips und ethisch-rechtliche Konsequenzen', in *Naturwissenschaftliche Rundschau*, 6, vol. 5, 2008, pp. 221–5.

29. Cf. L. Siep, *Konkrete Ethik, op. cit.*

Does the Natural-Law Approach have a Future? A Hermeneutical Proposal: Nine Objections to Natural Law

JEAN-PIERRE WILS

The language of natural law would appear to be subject to a number of ideological objections. In this article I shall cite only the most important elements of this critique.

(a) A supposed constancy of certain basic legal principles that is said to be inherent in natural law and is contrasted with the experience of the fundamental inconstancy of law proper to a modern context.

(b) A variation of this problematical aspect of the notion is the slowness or enduring validity characteristic of natural law, and this makes it an inappropriate instrument for moral and legal handling of questions arising in an expeditious society.

(c) Natural law is so abstract as to contradict the notion that law must allow practical outcomes.

(d) The concept of natural law always features confusion between facts and standards, whereas clear distinctions between them are needed on ethical as well as legal grounds.

(e) The further development and differentiation of natural law during the Enlightenment led to an additional complication: the equation of reason with nature runs entirely counter to the understanding of nature as the object of the interventionist exercise of reason.

(f) Natural law implies a certain universalism that is irreconcilable with a pluriformity of cultures and with the actual multiplicity of local moral and legal systems; with, that is, a requisite particularism.

(g) The distinctions between law and morality are too imprecisely delineated in the concept of natural law to be applied effectively in a complex and highly differentiated society.

(h) Natural law relies on a teleological conception of human nature that

cannot lay claim to any privileged position under the conditions of a radically de-teleologicalized view of nature in general.

(i) Natural law (at least in the sense of a supposedly immutable natural law) lays claim to what amounts to *a priori* status. In reality, the status of natural law is *a posteriori*, for it is the result of a protracted struggle to obtain standards that have proved valid in numerous situations of moral conflict.

The foregoing objections are extremely varied. To defend or attack them would demand much more extensive treatment than is possible in the present context. But some degree of differentiation is necessary from a historical as from a systematic viewpoint. Nevertheless, the above-mentioned objections show unmistakably that natural law is fatally susceptible to ideological criticism. I shall devote the rest of this article to an appropriately short discussion of the critique of natural law advanced by Niklas Luhmann, who is both sociologist and systems theoretician. Some of the nine objections will recur in the course of this representation, even if formulated differently to some extent. I shall treat the problem of universalism more specifically in the last part of the article. On the basis of some points made by Michael Walzer, I shall defend the thesis that the problem of universalism can be represented in the tradition of natural law, though only if the universalism in question here is conceived of hermeneutically.

I. Deconstruction of natural law: Niklas Luhmann

Niklas Luhmann is responsible for the proposition that 'human rights result from the deconstruction of natural law' (Luhmann 2005, 218f). Deconstruction in this context does not imply that human rights supersede natural law in a form compatible with modern thought, but that they reveal a problem inherent in natural law, and thereby take natural law further under different conditions. As soon as human rights are included in constitutional texts and benefit from the forms of stability guaranteed by a constitution, they become legally 'normalized' to some extent. This, however, Luhmann notes, gives rise to a 'paradox' – 'in the shape of prepositive law calling for a positive expression' (Luhmann 2005, 211). Human rights seem to share the fortunes of natural law. Natural law is also (so it seems permissible to maintain) 'normalized in the practice of modern, predominantly positive law'. But what exactly does this mean?

A modern development has led to the separation between morals and law. At the level of overall social control, the equation of law and morals in the concept of law (*lex*) becomes increasingly less meaningful. To put it in

Kantian terms, henceforth legal duties and virtuous duties are no longer virtually identical. Or, in terms proper to systems theory, we may say that 'Law is appropriate to the requirements of a functionally differentiated society, even if not to the dictates of humanity' (Luhmann 2006, 115). Here it is principally the concept of natural law that is subject to pressures to adapt, which ultimately force it to undergo radical transformations. From the viewpoint of a 'functionally differentiated society' with all its distinct subsystems of law, morality, religion, and politics, the idea of nature loses its control function. These subsystems rely on specific basic codes – the codes of justice and injustice, good and evil, salvation and calamity, and power and powerlessness – which essentially do not have to rely on any other codes but guarantee the (relative) autonomy of the relevant subsystem. The concept of nature becomes superfluous in the context of the subsystems in question. 'The decisive aspect of the concept of nature is . . . an extra-systemic accountability, amounting to a denial of the inherent causality of the accountable system – a logical expedient typical of still relatively simple systems' (Luhmann 2006, 186).

For a long time the notion of natural law has acted as a kind of parenthesis relating law to morals. But in both areas it has come to be seen increasingly as at best a mere embellishment that has lost all significance in the semantics of both social sub-systems. It is not essences but functions that are determinative in modern societies. Boundaries have to be drawn in the areas of law and morals – 'generalized behavioural expectations' or norms are required here of course, but now they are 'limits that no longer count as essential principles together with axioms conceived of as nature, but as normative regulations, legal obligations, expectations and priorities' (Luhmann 2006, 192). Natural law has a long history (with many twists and turns). But the stability often ascribed to natural law depends on a simplification. In this connection, Luhmann has referred to the nominalist critics of the Middle Ages, who had already impugned the stable bases of any future natural law both by reference to the will of God or to his power (*potestas*) on the one hand and to their anti-realist ontology on the other hand. Two quotations from Luhmann will suffice to show the specific relevance of this criticism.

'The Christian rehandling of the natural law of classical antiquity . . . was a significant process. It transferred the basis of all law from institutions to the will of God, from tradition to transcendence – and therefore almost to the level of theologically contentious principles. This made the kind of highly-nuanced abstraction which theologians used to discuss the absolute nature of divine omnipotence and its consequences for the natural order of the world relevant for law. Any considerable degree of uncertainty in the structure of law no longer found any support in religious fundamentals. . . . The separation of religion and law was already anticipated in the degree of abstraction proper to theological disputation. The idea that God created the law . . . made all law seem contingent, and open to other possibilities, and the next step was that creation had only to be transferred to the human subject, to reason, to conscience and to the legislator. . . . A theological grounding of the invariability of the contents of legal norms was no longer possible' (Luhmann 2006, 198).

Of course the observation that concentration on the will of God – and therefore on his ordaining power – already substantially anticipated the notion of positive law is of central importance here. The key notion in this case is contingency. But contingency meant that doubt had been sown in a highly dramatic way: doubt, that is, whether the possibility that there could be a different kind of law and morality (their contingency) could really still be reconciled with the idea of the essential invariability of legal standards. Furthermore, it seems wholly permissible to conclude that the pairing of law and creation in the concept of the creation of law opens up a whole range of possible associated notions, which then actually make their appearance as the suggestions proffered by Luhmann. Admittedly, this nominalist criticism was not entirely novel. Certain guiding principles were already available in the Sophist Enlightenment in ancient Greece. But the supreme effectiveness of the new critique cannot be overestimated. Even the association of will and contingency represents a decisive blow for natural law by advancing the idea that law depends on decision. Indeed, the later positivist make-over of law depends to a great extent on the concept of decision. The validity of the law is 'related to a variable factor . . . in fact to a decision'. Luhmann suggests that the law can be taken as positive only if the 'law is experienced as depending on this decision for its validity, as selected among other possibilities, and therefore as subject to change. The historically new and daring aspect of the positive character of the law is the legitimization of changes in the law' (Luhmann 2006, 209).

It is not difficult to suppose that that any such 'legalization of changes in the law' must enter into direct conflict with the idea that the law, at least in its fundamentals, must embody a canon of basic moral rules traditionally held to be invariable. The debates about the relation of positive to prepositive or natural law illustrate the complex of problems at issue here. There should be no question that the detachment of law from morals does not imply that the law takes no account of morals. If law is permanently in conflict with moral

intuitions and convictions, it is experienced as injustice. But any more precise elucidation of the relationship between them is much more controversial. In fact it is not at all easy to answer the question 'whether the normative
validity of positive law means that it is necessarily subject to moral – or at
least to certain minimal moral – norms, which are then known as natural law;
or whether, in spite of the notional validity of all moral pre-standardization
of positive law, its binding nature requires no assistance and is independent
of any agreement or non-agreement with morality.'

In view of the temptation to avoid a supposed threat of arbitrariness or
relativism 'by referring to a residue of invariable basic elements; by, that is,
invoking at least some absolute values or a minimum number of ethical and
natural-law norms', Luhmann says that 'if however we insist on maintaining that reflexive mechanisms are essential to retain the achieved level of
social complexity, any such recourse to pre-reflexive notions of classification becomes questionable. The certainty that they seem to promise becomes
increasingly illusory. . . . They are not sufficiently directional to control the
process of ongoing structural variations effectively. They exclude too little,
and do not feature adequate clues to solutions that can be used in each specific
case. As a result of the very invariability ascribed to them, they are over-
stretched and become almost inconsequential. Accordingly, it is questionable whether the dimension and assurance of flexibility are still to be sought
effectively in inflexibility' (Luhmann 2006, 215f). This would appear to be
a (provisional) final judgment of natural law. Nevertheless, even this denial
of natural law offers us clues that might help us to defend one of its fundamental concerns. The relevant watchwords are 'inflexibility' and 'reflexive
mechanisms'. I shall now try to define their relation to the 'universalism'
found in every version of natural law.

II. A flexible universalism

In 'Nation and World', his short though influential paper of 1990, Michael
Walzer introduced a distinction between two kinds of universalism. First we
have 'covering-law universalism', which presumes the existence of a God
and – because and insofar as there is a God – a law, a justice, and a right
way of understanding the good life, the good society, or the good form of
government, a redemption and a Messiah (Walzer 1994). This universalism is actually deeply rooted in Jewish and Christian religion. Christianity,
yes, but also a major element of tradition in Judaism conceives of itself as
religion with a global political and therefore a universalist claim. Alongside

this, Judaism also features a second tradition that is not particularist in the strict sense of the word but also embraces no form of abstract universalism. Two passages in the Prophets Amos and Isaiah are decisive here: 'Are not you Israelites like the Cushites to me? . . . Did I not bring Israel up from Egypt, and the Philistines from Caphtor, the Aramaens from Kir?' (Amos 9 7). And: 'Blessed be Egypt, my people, Assyria my handiwork, and Israel my possession' (Isa. 19.25).

Both pronouncements from scripture are of decisive importance for Walzer and make it possible, in addition to the intended revaluation but also equalization of each specific nation, to perceive a comparable experience and a comparable destiny for each of them: the experience of repression and liberation (in the case of Amos) and God's loving-kindness (in the case of Isaiah). Experience and destiny are universal, but history and context are different and particular in each case. Therefore the universal does exist, but only in the mode of each repetition. Accordingly, Walzer talks of a 'reiterative universalism', and what distinguishes this from the 'universalism of the all-covering law' is its particularist viewpoint and pluralizing tendency (Walzer 1994). One might also speak here of that which is special or 'individually general' (Manfred Frank), since universalism is clearly observable only in the mode of its special or individual reiteration.

Walzer sees both forms of universalism so to speak as two historical options. Accordingly, in this case the references to Amos and Isaiah are not mere illustrations of moral-philosophical problems but provide insights into their historical origins and into their context, without which we could scarcely understand both forms of universalism. In both cases we learn something about the origin of moral principles. The universalism of the all-covering law is just as much the product of a particular history as reiterative universalism, but whereas the first subordinates the specific to the general and then as it were discards it, for the second universalism the specific is the starting-point and point of return, whereas the universal is that which is present in the mode of recognition in each local experience. Accordingly, the origin of principles also teaches us – insofar as we also profess an hermeneutical or interpretative approach – something about their validity. Whereas 'abstract' universalism lays claim to a validity that holds irrespective of context and should be applied as the individual case demands only as a secondary consideration, 'specific' universalism maintains that principles can exist and flourish only in specific and accordingly pluralistic settings. They acquire and express their validity only in context.

Here, too, Walzer sees the different traditions of Judaism as pointing in different ways. The burden of the monotheistic God is said to reside in his apparently essential association with abstract universalism. But Walzer constantly reminds us that there are so to speak heterodox traditions that insist on God's difference and complexity. Thereafter this viewpoint becomes characteristic of the subject of morality, for what human beings have in common is precisely this creative power, which is not the ability to do the same thing in the same way, but the ability to do many different things in different ways. It is the (faintly) reflected, distributed and particularized omnipotence of God. Accordingly, it is only meaningful to speak of a moral self if we attribute sufficient behavioural areas to this self within which it can operate: that is, sufficient contexts in which, in cultural and social particularity, it can make general principles and categories visible and comprehensible as it recalls them. We have to remember that all-inclusive laws or a collection of laws providing an appropriately complete basis for our work simply do not exist. Moreover, it is useless trying to substitute a substantial imitation for the authentic process of recall (Walzer 1994).

Against this background Walzer is able to offer a concise but also surprising moral-philosophical explanation of the relation between universalism and particularism. Moral concepts (and principles too) can have a minimal and a maximal meaning in each case. Depending on the context, such notions are inclined to be 'thin' or 'thick'. Because we live in actual specifically meaningful contexts with social, political, and cultural implications, our concepts also reflect these conditions of life closely. They do so normally, for in conflict situations, that is, in abnormal existential contexts, we tend to sharpen our concepts and principles so that they become more abstract or thinner. In cases of conflict we refer, for instance, to justice as such, or to human dignity as such. This interim 'minimalism' contains what we tend to 'acknowledge repeatedly', which means a certain mutuality, even though otherwise we exist in entirely different settings in which specifically or 'maximalistically' determined concepts may have other meanings and applications in any particular case.

Walzer says that he sees minimal morality as the sum of everything that we repeatedly acknowledge. He stresses the fact that minimalism does not describe a morality that is lower in content or emotionally shallow, for the opposite is true: minimal morality is morality pure and simple. Scarcely anything is more important than truth and justice understood minimally in that way. As soon as anyone refuses the minimal requirements that we demand of each other in a social context, they are repeated passionately and insistently. Shallowness and intensity go hand in hand in moral discourse, whereas thick or dense description means that restrictions, complexity, and differences of opinion are involved as well (Walzer 1994). Nevertheless, it is no easy matter to separate 'thin' from 'thick' concepts and principles. The universalism of 'thin', minimalist ideas refers to a divided humankind, and the particularism of 'thick', maximalist ideas refers to the place, to the actual society, in which we live in each specific case. But universalism can be detected only in particular lived moral worlds. Accordingly, the belief that particularism must be preceded by a universal, minimalist fundamental morality that is binding on everyone and which everyone can understand is false, for maximalism precedes minimalism. The importance of this fact for a hermeneutical approach cannot be underestimated. After all, those who advance the common philosophical assumption that a universalist minimal morality must come first and only later has to be made specific and then applied, would have first of all to explain how and why people can possibly manage to understand and implement any such supposedly primary minimal morality in the first place. If, as Walzer says, we do nevertheless understand the abstract notion of minimal morality, this is attributable to the fact that it is derived from a specific historical constellation (Walzer 1994)

Consequently hermeneutical experience enjoys a certain primacy as far as morality is concerned. Clearly, there are historical and cultural contexts within which our moral discourse originates. All those terms which we use to talk about morals have a specific origin. But the fact that the effective application of this moral language is also unavoidably contextualized is associated with the realization that this is the only way in which we can understand what we do anyway. Walzer is reluctant to talk of 'relativism' too in such contexts, although only a partial relativism would be involved here. After all, the universalist aspect of minimal morality is a major component of such contexts. This internal universalism is repeated in those situations in which the contexts are temporarily conflictual. But we would be out of kilter with the minimal morality that we operate in those conflicts and tension situations if we were not to exercise it constantly in the maximalist version of morals. Therefore the path of moral philosophy to be followed is the 'way of interpretation', and neither the 'way of discovery', as for instance with moral concepts derived from a revelation, nor the 'way of invention' that would mislead us into constructive procedures (as in the case, for example, of Rawls and Habermas), the outcome of which we might use as a yardstick for the life of any individual and for the practices of any society (Walzer 1987). Accordingly, to aim at viewing the moral world from no specific viewpoint (cf. Nagel 1970 and 1986), as is usual in the process of construction, would be equivalent to devising a moral Esperanto, a lifeless artificial language that would tend to idealize that moral world. The following account should make Walzer's own approach especially clear.

Walzer argues that an interpretation is a judgment and therefore represents the operation of a specific judicial force. Interpretation may be said to advance a claim based on the assumption that neither discovery nor invention is necessary, because we already possess what they purport to offer us. Morality differs from politics in that it requires neither executive power nor systematic legislation. We do not have to discover the moral world, for that is where we have always been living. We do not have to invent it, because it has already been invented – if not in accordance with this or that specific philosophical methodology. The design of the moral world was not subservient to any process of construction, and the result, though admittedly unstructured and uncertain, is certainly very much there. The moral world has a lived-in quality and the entire edifice – viewed as a whole – may be compared not so much to an abstract model as to a dense description. Moral argumentation in such an environment takes on more of the character of an interpretation; indeed, it may be said to approach the condition of a barrister's or judge's work, when he or she is trying to find a meaning in a morass of conflicting laws and precedents (Walzer 1994).

This viewpoint is impressively reminiscent of the tradition of moral philosophy (and rhetoric) since Aristotle, according to which moral judgments issue from a topical and referentially orientated interpretation of specific cases, so that those judgments are indeed firmly anchored in the compact setting of their origin, yet at the same time their status is just as much that of mere probability. Walzer justly maintains that a moral judgment is so to speak the provisional result of a complex interpretation and represents the 'meaning' of a moral conflict against the background of an actual specific social or cultural constellation. To a certain extent, the 'discovery' (the executive function) comes too late, for the laws have already been promulgated a long time before; the 'invention' (the legislative function) does indeed arrive too late, for those to whom it is addressed have been living in compact moral worlds for a long time, and the more specific the codification becomes in this respect, the more closely it approaches the category of 'interpretation', and accordingly the more judgmental it is. Consequently, moral argumentation *in casu* is Walzer's initial model. We start arguing as soon as we find it no longer possible to classify a case without difficulty, and from the point at which our traditional moral understanding is somehow blocked. To escape this obstruction, we engage in a consultation, in the deliberative course of which the existing laws, principles, and categories are subjected to a critical stocktaking. But this kind of examination calls neither for a new nor for a detached ethics that goes to work irrespective of tradition and with something like revisionist fervour.

Of course Walzer would not seek to deny the existence of universal and minimal sets of prohibitions, or minor codices of elementary negative obligations. But he reminds us quite properly that they too were neither discovered nor invented. We have to think of them as prohibitions that came about little by little, and as the result of many years of trial and error and of constantly failing, partial, and uncertain comprehension (Walzer 1987). Accordingly, the process of forming a moral judgment, like the process of moral codification, occurs in three stages. First, understanding is obstructed by a novel, highly conflictual situation. Then the problem is identified against the background of existing interpretations necessarily affected by tradition. Finally, the case is modified in the course of a new, critical interpretation. Furthermore, the above-mentioned sets of prohibitions also have to be subjected repeatedly to hermeneutical analysis in the light of reiterative universalism. Their apparently universalist minimalism first occurs, as we have seen, in maximalist versions and finally re-enters these multifarious versions. In this sense we might actually conclude that the approaches known as discovery and invention are ultimately no more than concealed or incompetent and etiolated interpretations.

How can we profitably apply the results of this summary account of Walzer's ideas to the problem of natural law? Our discussion of the question of universalism has supplied us with the insight that similar, though not equivalent, experiences lead to the construction of certain principles – fundamental rules of universalist import – to express that which is common to those similar experiences, while intermittently disregarding what is divisive or specific in each new experience. The principles may be seen as highly sensitive yardsticks for assessing crisis situations, if we understand a crisis here as a (temporary) lack of any appropriately practical moral judgment. Walzer's 'reiterated universalism' fully appreciates the fact that even those principles we subject to a kind of *a priori* rationality result from an actual and therefore specific history, which is often a history of suffering. They are jointly and severally *a posteriori*. Natural-law principles too can be seen thus, and stand at (once again a provisional) end to a conflict about interpretation. They summarize what has been shown to be valid hitherto. But in new situations we shall have to invest them anew in the argument about a new interpretation. It is difficult to suppose that proven principles could be entirely divested of their validity in any such argument. But it will be necessary over and again to reconstruct their meaning, and their understanding, which will be wrested from whatever the specific conflict situations happen to be. In this way natural law becomes versatile, reflexive, and capable of responding to some of the objections formulated at the beginning of this article. Clearly there is an inheritance from natural law that persists beyond natural law.

Translated by J. G. Cumming

Further reading

Niklas Luhmann, 'Das Paradox der Menschenrechte und drei Formen seiner Entfaltung', in *Soziologische Aufklärung 6. Die Soziologie und der Mensch*, Wiesbaden, ²2005, pp. 218–25.

Niklas Luhmann, *Rechtssoziologie*, Wiesbaden, ⁴2008.

Thomas Nagel, *The View from Nowhere*, New York & Oxford, 1986.

Thomas Nagel, *The Possibility of Altruism*, Princeton, 1970.

Michael Walzer, *Interpretation and Social Criticism*, Cambridge, Mass. & London, 1987.

Michael Walzer, *Thick and Thin. Moral Argument at Home and Abroad*, Notre Dame, 1994.

Feminist Natural Law

CRISTINA TRAINA

Why would any self-respecting Catholic feminist continue to defend a natural law approach to ethics? In the twelve years since my first defence,[1] Roman Catholic ecclesiastical teaching has continued its trend toward the evangelical counsels and away from the liberal, Enlightenment-tinged reason that has captivated Anglo-American Catholics. In the same period, many secular feminist scholars have continued their double paths toward feminine essentialism on one hand and a vision of gender as entirely a social construction on the other. Natural law seems weirdly out of place in both of these conversations, especially when one remembers how often it has been used to stifle intellectual exchange, justify oppressive hierarchies, and encourage political quietism. Nothing about it seems either inspiring or liberating.

And yet I contend, as other authors in this issue have often argued, that the foundational theology, epistemology, and method of Roman Catholic natural law are not only congenial to feminist ethics but perhaps necessary to Christian versions of it.[2] Applied honestly to contemporary society, they often lead to different conclusions than natural law had traditionally reached, a phenomenon that requires us to think of the world as subject to some unchanging limits but also as dynamic within those boundaries. Thus I argue that a critical, self-critical version of natural law combines the potential for confident advocacy for justice (based on enduring limits) with intellectual humility (rooted in responsiveness to changing events and evolving knowledge). This, I think, is the truthful and genuine combination in a society that is undergoing constant intellectual expansions and upheavals and yet is still in need of reliable, prophetic, decisive work on behalf of the marginalized.

I. Thomistic natural law

The most basic definition of the natural law in Thomas Aquinas's *Summa Theologiae* is 'the rational creature's participation of the eternal law' (II–II

91.2), which is 'the very Idea of the government of things' in God's providence (II–II 91.1). God's providence, in turn, creates human beings for
beatitude, for perfection in and union with God. This providence is aimed at
eternal life but embraces the physical and social character of human beings.
Thus it is organized so that our moral, intellectual, spiritual, and physical
flourishing are coherent and, to a degree, mutually dependent in the long
run. For instance, although our salvation is by no means dependent on our
physical welfare, if our physical and social needs are fulfilled not just minimally, but more generously and flexibly, we can more easily 'be becomingly'
(for example, II–II 141.6.2) in all dimensions of our lives.[3] In addition, God's
providence ensures that personal, communal, and even global flourishing
are generally coherent if we organize communities, societies, and even international relations so that they promote and protect all the dimensions of
flourishing. Finally, we have faith, based in revelation, that God intends us
to flourish holistically. Consequently, reasoning about flourishing is practical, pursuing a particular vision of the good life informed by revelation; it
is also inductive, asking what habits, acts, structures, and qualities promote
that vision or cause it harm.

In addition, Thomas recognizes that sin has much to do with our failure to
flourish. Sin undermines God's providence, in which natural law shares, by
subverting the 'best practices' that God has set up for our welfare. When we
use these practices well, flourishing usually results; when we use them badly
or ignore them, harm tends to follow. Yet despite his reputation for inflexibility, Thomas never implies that there is only one right way to accomplish
flourishing. Diet varies by climate, health, and personality; there is more
than one workable form of government; local custom plays a large rule in
human law, even within the universal natural law's criteria for justice.

This practical, realistic flexibility of natural law is worth re-emphasis in
the face of recent trends in papal ethics. Pope John Paul II's embrace of the
evangelical counsels was inspiring but tended to dismiss the pressures of
intimate and structural sin as irrelevant to personal moral decisions, and
even to political decision-making in some cases. Pope Benedict XVI is still
revealing his ethical trajectory, but it is not clear that his identification of
truth and goodness (certainly ontologically correct) will not substitute speculative knowledge for the inductive processes upon which natural law insists
for practical reasoning.

What, then, is problematic about Thomas' vision of natural law? Despite
his affirmations of variety and flexibility, Thomas assumes that because God's
providence is changeless the central content of humanity's participatory

practical reasoning is changeless as well: natural law is a stable quantity that simply comes into greater focus gradually over time, with only slight local adaptations in application. Neither God's provident wisdom nor the conclusions of human participation in it ever changes appreciably.[4] Apparent significant reversals (like Jesus' repeal of God's permission for Israelite polygamy) ended temporary divine concessions to sin but did not alter God's original intent; they were certainly not based on new, inductive, reasoned reflection about the changed social conditions for holistic flourishing in first-century Palestine in comparison with the Abrahamic period. For Thomas reflective human experience simply never contradicts – because it cannot contradict – the firm conclusions of natural law already laid down.

As many of the authors in this issue have also noted, among these changeless conclusions, the 'best practices' that Thomas embraces include universal hierarchies of gender, class, vocation, and other factors in which the categorically superior rule over the categorically inferior. That is, relationships of domination and subordination based on divinely-intended differences in excellence are essential to the ordered harmony on which human communal flourishing depends. This conviction clearly runs counter to feminist visions of justice and flourishing.

II. Feminist natural law

Feminist natural law embraces every point I have mentioned except those in the preceding two paragraphs. For feminists as for Thomas, holistic flourishing – and systematic opportunities for it – are essential measures of justice, and the many elements and scales of flourishing are interdependent. Christian feminism depends absolutely on the conviction that although biological gender occasionally inflects the concrete preconditions of human flourishing (simple examples: women need access to pre-natal care and maternity leave, but men do not; men need access to prostate cancer screening, but women do not), God's providence includes the full, holistic flourishing of all human beings individually and in community. For feminism (as for all thought based on liberationist principles) the welfare of those most marginalized in society is the measure of that society's success in promoting the common good: individual and communal holistic flourishing. That welfare includes not only personal thriving but the capacity to contribute constructively and thoughtfully to the social, political good. Consequently, flourishing implies a lack of rigid hierarchy and demands tolerance of a certain degree of flux and 'disorder.'

Feminists are, if possible, more aware of the obstacles that sin creates for flourishing than traditional natural law thinkers might be. In particular, hierarchical social systems and customs can be toxic, and their toxicity can afflict individual lives on a grand scale in ways that are not simply a matter of material suffering. The benefit of feminism's realism about sin is a non-complacent search for the violence and oppression that apparently peaceful order can hide. For instance, societies that forbid education to women stunt their political and social participation. A political and economic situation in which survival demands a habit of dishonesty and manipulation warps or 'burdens' virtue so that 'the mode of survival in this place and time' does not match the shape of a virtuous life in more congenial circumstances.[5] Thomas's solution – for example, that taking another's possessions when one is in desperate need is not sinful (ST II–II 66.7) – does not quite capture this insight. Feminist scholars dedicate themselves not only to correcting glaring injustice but to looking under the surface continually to determine whether injustice resides there unnoticed and uncriticized, perpetuating itself in burdened virtues and dysfunctional systems.

A feminist approach to natural law also amplifies Thomas's dicta about variety and change in application of natural law. Most basically, it embraces Thomas's dictum that the secondary precepts vary according to time, place, and person because the practical requirements of holistic flourishing, and therefore of the means of virtue, are different in each situation. For instance, I know that if I do not exercise vigorously several times every week, a depression will descend that makes it all but impossible for me to cooperate with God's charity, with unpleasant consequences for me and all those close to me. But your holistic flourishing may have slightly different preconditions. This individuality is one source of variety and change.

As Thomas did, we must make use of the sciences and social sciences to analyze the conditions that seem to promote flourishing generally. And, like Thomas, we know that deeper insight often alters our understanding of the 'same' phenomenon. This evolving, scientifically-driven vision is a second source of variety and change.

Unlike Thomas, however, we also realize that the pursuit of scientific truth is always biased in one way or another and must be analyzed critically: for instance, studies designed to teach us about *human* disease and healing have increasingly been revealed to illuminate the flourishing of most adult *men* but not of women or children. In addition, although scientific method is continuous and relatively consistent, scientific knowledge is not precisely cumulative; new discoveries constantly qualify or even reverse the correlations and causes we thought we knew, even introducing new paradigms for the creation that we believe reveals elements of God's providence. If we truly believe in the coherence of practical, moral, and spiritual flourishing, our understandings of human goods and even of virtues must be open to transformation on the basis of what we learn inductively.

Thus precisely because it is keenly aware of the biases that limited experience can introduce into the reasoning of whatever group happens to be culturally ascendant, feminist ethics is sceptical that honest, inductive reflection will always confirm the wisdom of the past. That is, participation in God's providence should lead to an ambitious, inductive, practical epistemology of self-critical humility rather than over-confidence. No matter how much we think we already know, we need always to be busy discerning what constitutes flourishing and how to promote it, in particular for people who are in any way marginalized. Even more importantly, we must let them speak first and freely, and we must be prepared to have our assumptions challenged.

Finally, as many authors in this volume have also argued, a Thomistic theological anthropology envisions the same heavenly beatitude and the same earthly virtues for all. It cannot coherently support the belief that women – or any other class of people – are categorically inferior, intended by God to be less capable than others of holistic flourishing and destined to be subordinate to others throughout their lives. As Jean Porter has written, we must choose Thomas's central theological anthropology and his method over his less generous conclusions.[6] We must insist that individuals – and perhaps even classes of individuals – may turn out to accomplish this holism in different styles; but variations in personality and circumstance that are not the products of sin and injustice are opportunities for, rather than divinely mandated limits upon, the forms that flourishing may take.

III. What about post-modern thought?

I have been arguing that natural law ought not be considered a true opponent of feminism. The key distinction here is self-critical, ongoing use of natural law method rather than embrace of past natural law conclusions. The greater challenges to natural law feminism are thus various post-modern moves in Western thought. In crucial respects, I believe, they fail to defeat the arguments I have been making, although they must be accounted for.

The position that all social identities, beliefs, visions of flourishing, and institutions are the outcomes of social power is compelling in an era of profound global and historical awareness. It is also an indispensable tool for critical ethical reflection. But it is not a sufficient tool. Lacking stable referents, this approach can reliably criticize an ethic. It shines a harshly critical light on our actions and ideals, helpfully revealing the problematic mix of motives that underlies social mores. But it cannot produce an ethic. It provides no critical leverage for an argument that we should stay or change the course, and it can generate no vision of the good unsullied by problematic, self-interested use of social power. Likewise, philosophies of essentialism and radical otherness honour the deep differences of experience, perspective, and wisdom that characterize us in a diverse world, but they have difficulty explaining how we should collaborate and toward what good common end. They can also be limiting, forbidding individuals to transcend their groups and identities.

Feminist natural-law thought has the advantage of combining the postmodern capacity for rigorous, inductive, open-ended criticism with a substantive if flexible vision of the good and a moral mandate to pursue it, for oneself and others. Through commitment to holistic flourishing and to inductive reflection, it embraces both the traditionalist view that our bodies and the natural world in some sense encode information about God's provident desires for us and the post-modern view that bodies and their goods are for better and worse socially constructed. What we 'see the body as' profoundly affects how we treat it. Even more pressingly, how we treat the body socially turns out to affect who we are emotionally and spiritually, and even to affect our genes. For instance, we now know that the way we interact with infants socially affects their growth and probably even their brain structure, permanently affecting their future flourishing.[7] In addition, we know that our cultural eating habits can affect the workings of the genes that can produce or prevent type II diabetes.[8] Individual virtue and personal and communal flourishing are connected, and often they are connected literally through physical bodies.

Thus natural-law feminism's concrete contribution to the post-modern discussion is that human social embodiment contains within itself opportunities and limits that in turn set shapes and boundaries to the still-infinite variations upon flourishing.[9] We are aiming at the good, for individuals and for humanity corporately; that good has a content, which we are forever discovering and which determines the broad boundaries that the conditions of our being create for us. The growing list includes bodily, intellectual, emotional, and spiritual health; social and political relations; developmental concerns; and environmental sustainability. For example, as Christine Gudorf has argued, 'humans cannot be human without relations to other humans'[10] and to the variable social structures and institutions that these connections demand. In addition, although biology never has the last word in human relations of any kind, social construction 'does not imply a total plasticity'[11] either. There are ways of being that force our bodies and our spirits out of balance with themselves and each other. Our social interactions are loosely constituted by our bodies and minds as well. For example, we cannot contradict the 'certain inner structures' of embodied human relating 'that predispose humans to seek patterns and order and to rely on them for fulfilling tasks.'[12] To flourish is to respect our character as inevitably social, embodied, rational, spiritual beings.

To respect our character means also to understand these relations in order to protect and promote them. As William Mattison has pointed out, natural law is practical reason. It strives for the good rather than generating the good. It must commit itself to a particular vision of the good before it can proceed.[13] What feminist natural law adds to this argument is the claim that our commitment to the good of holistic flourishing is real, but our insight into this good is nonetheless limited, evolving, and inductive, affected by our histories and our social positions, inflected by the needs of our situations.

I have hinted that one objection rooted in post-modern experience does stick, and it is one that any credible feminist natural-law theory must take to heart: the elements of flourishing are rarely harmonious in practice. Because of its emphasis on the repair of injustice and the healing of injury, feminism forbids us to forget that personal sin, the vagaries of nature, larger geopolitical systems, and just plain bad luck often converge in such a way that the varieties and scales of flourishing are literally incompatible in a particular time and place. Trade-offs must be made.

Here too we must follow the logical trail of Thomas's central commitments rather than accept his conclusions uncritically. Thomas often appears to handle conflicts by backing down from the ideal of holistic flourishing, in part because his vision of heavenly beatitude did not include the earthly body, Thomas tended to prefer the soul's good to the body's good; because of his convictions about hierarchy, he tended to prefer an orderly if unjust State to a disorderly one; and so on. And yet time and time again Thomas returned to the idea that physical self-preservation is the most basic element of the natural law (ST I-II 94.2) and that pursuit of one's own beatitude trumps all other ends. Thomas assumed that social and political relations would not realize the goals that participation in God's providence implies; circumstances would be imperfect; holistic flourishing would not always, or even usually, be possible in the moment. And yet virtuous action must still be within reach. Self-preservation, whether physical or spiritual, was the virtuous response, for the individual and for the State.

Natural-law feminism too must embrace self-preservation under duress as virtuous: women's self-defence against battering partners, for instance. And yet we must insist that 'burdened' virtues like these are not ideal, that it is not enough simply to say 'it is no sin' or 'it is good' for a woman to defend herself. Natural law feminism implies an eschatologically-driven dedication to establishing justice in the world: the material, social, and political right relations that will reduce such conflicts, lessening the burdens on virtue that arise from individual and corporate sinfulness.

An honest feminist natural law theory must also admit that human life in society will never resemble a perfectly balanced gyroscope, even assuming that humans are universally virtuous; it is buffeted by too many factors. Both natural events and the very critical and self-critical methods we employ to understand flourishing and establish justice create a dynamism that in itself will produce jarring moments. Randomness, incompleteness, change, and even growth – and not just direct attacks on the good – can produce suffering and conflict. Flourishing depends on the dynamic, ongoing capacity for maintaining – or regaining – holistic balance. Preconditions for a good life on both the personal and the social scale include the external resources and internal resiliency for keeping one's balance when these forces impinge. This is where our energy must lie: in doggedly insisting on the background conditions of welfare and political justice that make the collaborative project of flourishing possible.

Notes

1. Cristina L. H. Traina, *Feminist Ethics and Natural Law: The End of the Anathemas*, Washington, DC: Georgetown University Press, 1998.
2. Among the established feminist ethicists who have embraced versions of this position, I think in particular of Lisa Sowle Cahill, Diana Fritz Cates, Margaret Farley, Christine E. Gudorf, Patricia Beattie Jung, Susan Frank Parsons, and Jean Porter.
3. See for example Jean Porter, 'Chastity as a Virtue', *Scottish Journal of Theology* 58 no. 3 (2005), 285–301.
4. The impulse to reduce natural law to a list of increasingly refined, changeless rules is modern, not medieval (see William C. Mattison III, 'The Changing Face of Natural Law: The Necessity of Belief for Natural Law Norm Specification', *The Journal of the Society of Christian Ethics* 27 no. 1 [Summer 2007], 251–77).

Still, Thomas believed that most changes in natural law's conclusions were matters of further specification or application; subtractions – reversals of earlier conclusions – occur 'in some particular cases of rare occurrence' only (ST I-II 94.5).

5. Lisa Tessman, *Burdened Virtues: Virtue Ethics for Liberatory Struggles*, Studies in Feminist Philosophy, ed. Cheshire Calhoun, New York: OUP, 2005.

6. Jean Porter, 'At the Limits of Liberalism: Thomas Aquinas and the Prospects for a Catholic Feminism', *Theology Digest* 41 no. 4 (Winter 1994), 315–30.

7. See the sources in Cristina L. H. Traina, 'Touch on Trial: Power and the Right to Physical Affection', *Journal of the Society of Christian Ethics* 25 no. 1 (2005), 3–34.

8. 'Don't Blame Your Genes: They May Simply Be Getting Bad Instructions – From You', *The Economist* (5 Sept. 2009), print edition, at http://www.economist.com/sciencetechnology/displaystory.cfm?story_id=14350157 , last accessed 22 Sept. 2009.

9. For the argument that a post-modern ethics must balance its attention to culture with attention to 'nature', see Douglas Kellner, 'Zygmunt Bauman's Postmodern Turn', *Theory, Culture, and Society* 15 no. 1 (1998), 73–86.

10. Christine E. Gudorf, 'The Social Construction of Sexuality: Implications for the Churches', in *God Forbid: Religion and Sex in American Public Life*, ed. Kathleen M. Sands, New York: OUP, 2000, pp. 42–59, here 44.

11. Gudorf, 'Social Construction', p. 47.

12. Gudorf, 'Social Construction', p. 44.

13. See Mattison, 'Changing Face'.

Human Rights from an Asian Perspective: The Challenge of Diversity and the Limits to Universality

MARIA CHRISTINA ASTORGA

This paper sets out to answer the general question: 'Are the concepts of human nature, human goods, and natural law useful concepts in Asia?' Answering initially not as broadly as originally stated, I limit my focus to human rights and engage in a human rights discourse from an Asian perspective. I first establish the relation of human rights to natural law and then proceed to develop the two parts of the paper that discuss two issues around its main topic or theme. First is the issue of how the doctrine of human rights and its theological validation/justification within its original Scholastic framework is brought into the immensely diverse Asian context. Second is the issue of cultural specificity and universality in relation to an approach to human rights that claims to be Asian. As a whole, the paper seeks to offer critical insights on human rights from an Asian perspective.

I. From natural law to human rights

Natural law teaching and human rights doctrine are not synonymous, so I see it as a mistaken assumption to move directly from the concept of natural law from the Scholastic period to the idea of human rights in the modern period. Until recently the historiography of human rights held that there was a break between the medieval and the modern periods precisely on the emergence of human rights doctrine. This view asserts that, while human rights doctrine may have drawn on the ethos and language of earlier natural law theories, it is a distinctively modern creation with a decisively new emphasis on the claims of the individual.[1] This view has recently been challenged by the medievalist Brian Tierney in his groundbreaking work on the medieval origins of natural rights doctrine. He claims that the language and substance of this doctrine can be traced as far back as the thirteenth century.[2]

88

Jean Porter demonstrates this view, which she herself holds, by backtracking, that is by approaching human rights doctrine by way of returning to natural law teaching, focusing on the way the Scholastics dealt with the issue of how the two are fundamentally connected. The development of the natural law tradition by the Scholastics was informed by a wide range of perspectives, including classical, Jewish, and Christian approaches. Through selective interpretation and synthesis, they developed their theology in a new and distinctive way, with a fundamental commitment to the internal coherence of scripture and its congruence with other authoritative texts. This commitment led them to formulate a primary and paradigmatic concept of natural law as an interior power or capacity for moral discernment – a concept that was anticipated by the Stoics, who said that there is within the human person a force that discerns the objective natural law pervading the whole universe. For the Scholastics, this force took on a decisive shift of meaning and emphasis as something inherent, a subjective power or faculty directed by reason toward self autonomy.[3]

What precisely is this decisive shift? The Scholastics saw natural law not only as a force within persons that connects them to an objective order that makes a claim on their obligation, but also as a force on which they themselves have a claim, if they choose to, as directed by the imperative of reason and discernment, which results in the levelling of persons *qua* persons in terms of freedom and autonomy. Tierney expresses this shift of meaning of natural law as viewed by the Scholastics:

> If we are to find an earlier origin for natural rights theories we need to look for patterns of language in which *jus naturale* meant not only natural law or cosmic harmony, but also a faculty or ability or power of individual persons, associated with reason and moral discernment, defining an area of liberty where the individual was free to act as he pleased, leading on to specific claims and powers of humans *qua* humans.[4]

He points out that this way of understanding natural law did not necessarily imply a doctrine of natural rights but laid the foundation for developing such a doctrine. Jean Porter added that the 'decisive shift' that Tierney identifies was not just shaped by the social conditions of the twelfth and thirteenth centuries but was informed by scripture and Christian theology, as the Scholastics understood their tasks in their light. The capacity of the person for self-direction and mastery over one's own choices is not just one among many of human capacities but is that which distinctively constitutes the human person as image of God. The irreducible value and inviolability of each person – man, woman, and child, including sinners as well as the righteous, and even the damned – as image of God, reflected in their rational freedom and self-direction, lay at the foundation of the human rights doctrine.[5]

II. The challenge of diversity: the call for a perspectival dialogue

If Tierney's position is agreed, as Porter does, then the evolution of the doctrine of human rights from natural law should be understood not as a break but as a development of the tendencies and inclinations of the thirteenth century. But this claim would not be welcomed by other defenders of the human rights doctrine. Their backgrounds and contexts do not attune them to the theological framing of the foundations of human rights doctrine in the person as self-directing and self-autonomous by virtue of his/her being human, there where God's image is embodied. The theological validation of human rights doctrine is not assumed by most contemporary human rights scholars and activists.

While some human rights defenders may grant that these rights could have developed historically out of theological claims, they would not grant that the historical connection is necessary for their emergence. They do not hold that the doctrine has to be theologically grounded to be valid. In fact, it might be the case that it could be generated on other grounds, which are entirely secular. But as it is, I would contend, based on the sources cited above, that the doctrine of natural rights was developed in Western Europe and framed in theological terms. However, it was progressively abstracted from its theological validation and presented as secular to invite universal acclaim in pluralistic societies. What originally emerged within a specific theological context has been adapted and appropriated in new contexts and held up as approximately a universal moral law. Here we see that what originated from the context of European theologians and philosophers was adapted and appropriated in other contexts as a basis and standard and over time became the patrimony of the race.[6]

Questions, however, remain with regard to the context of human rights doctrine. Why should this doctrine, which was conceived in a specific theological context, be given a trans-cultural, trans-religious, universal validity? Insofar as it represents a specific religious culture, would it not be some kind of cultural or religious imperialism to hold it up as a basis for critique and reform for other contexts? What is the basis of its claims?

These questions become acute in the context of Asia with its immense diversity. Spanning large geographic areas, it is where 60 percent of the world's population lives. It is the locus of different cultures and religions, diverse political entities (States), and unevenly developed or underdeveloped economies and political systems. This is a heterogeneity that extends to its people, their social-political practices, and ethnic cultural identities. This heterogeneity of Asia particularly extends to its religions, which to a very large extent have shaped its culture. All the world's major religions are represented in Asia: Christianity in the Philippines, Islam in Malaysia, Hinduism in Nepal, and Buddhism in Sri Lanka and Thailand.[7]

Beyond this great diversity of religions is the diversity of political systems, which range from semi-feudal kingdoms in Kuwait and Saudi Arabia, through military systems in Burma and Cambodia, effectively one-party regimes in Singapore and Indonesia, communist regimes in China and Vietnam, and democracies in the Philippines, Malaysia, Sri Lanka, and India. Running through all these systems are different ideologies such as socialism, democracy, or feudalism, which animate governments and peoples. The economic circumstances in Asian countries are as diverse as their religious and political circumstances. Japan, Singapore, and Hong Kong are among the world's most prosperous countries, while there is grinding poverty in Bangladesh, India, and the Philippines. The diversity of economic circumstances reflects the diversity of economic systems that govern these countries, which range from tribal subsistence economies in parts of Indonesia to the highly-developed market economies of Singapore, Hong Kong, and Taiwan, the mixed economy model of India, and the planned economies of China and Vietnam.[8]

Given this immense and complex plurality of human realities and conditions in Asia, one can very well see how any declaration of human rights with a theological validation, when couched in a religious language belonging to a specific religious tradition, can be challenged. Specifically, this is the challenge of declarations on human dignity and rights by the Catholic Church when addressed to peoples of different religious worldviews and ideological allegiances. What is needed here is a dialogue of perspectives where people of different religious traditions and secular orientations come to bring their own visions of a good life. In an active perspectival dialogue, across boundaries of religion and culture, people of diverse worldviews enter into communities of understanding and solidarity, even there where differences may not be completely overcome.[9]

'What Jacques Dupuis says about the providential function of the diversity of religions may well be applied to the diversity of moral traditions as well . . . preserving distinctive forms of human goodness which could not be captured in any one overarching moral system, however admirable and just.'[10] This perspectival dialogue envisions arriving at a 'compelling core of shared values' with a vocabulary and codification that may vary across a wide span of contexts and worldviews. In this dialogue, human rights doctrine that rests on theological grounds may express a most fundamental value whose attraction and persuasion may have a moral resonance in the hearts of people who may not share its presuppositions, much less its language and expression.

III. The limits to universality of human rights: toward a culturally inclusive universalism

Most will hold that in order to make a plausible case for the universality of 'rights' claims, it is necessary to couch such claims in very general terms. As Annette Baier remarks, 'Lists of universal rights, if they are both to cohere and to receive anything like general assent, must be so vague as to be virtually empty.'[11] In the same vein, Jean Porter writes that 'the more we specify what we mean by a right, the more difficult it becomes to offer convincing answers to someone who finds the relevant right claims to be unpersuasive or morally unjustified.'[12]

She says that it is hard to see how anyone can oppose the fundamental right to human dignity, but when this right is made more specific as to the right of a religious dissident to his beliefs and practice or the right of a woman to wear or not to wear her veil, a contentious situation is created.[13]

But it is not only the case of specifying universal claims to rights that creates problems and raises issues. Interpreting, adapting, and adjudicating these universal rights in different contexts produce the same outcomes. The Bangkok Declaration of 1993 constituted the most serious challenge to the universal normative claims of human rights. Countries of East Asia (Singapore, Malaysia, Indonesia, and China) increasingly self-assured as a result of tremendous economic growth, asserted their place in the global discourse on human rights. They denounced the self-righteousness of the Western States, which preach about human rights when they were responsible for the colonial legacy of rights abuses in the Asian countries over which they now sit in judgment. They asserted that human rights must reflect the particular economic and political circumstances of each country.[14] This stance was reflected in the Chinese White Paper, which states: 'Owing to tremendous differences in historical background, social system, cultural tradition, and economic development, countries differ in their understanding of human rights.'[15]

The thrust of the Asian values argument is the claim that Asia can pose a counter-model to the Western way of life as it prioritizes community over the individual, social rights over civil and political rights, and social order and stability over democracy and freedom. This counter-model, which relies on the strong hand of a wise and benevolent patriarch, can succeed by instilling Asian values of obedience, thrift, industriousness, respect for elders and authority, emphasis on family, and restraint of immediate gratification. Also, Asian societies are said to proceed by 'consensus' and not by conflict, favouring cooperative rather than coercive measures for human rights.[16] This Asian approach to human rights is defined by a paradigm of development termed as 'liberty trade-off' or the 'Lee Kuan Yew hypothesis', which holds that Asian governments are justified in denying their people their civil and political rights in favour of social stability and economic growth.[17]

Not surprisingly, the contentious and provocative claims of Asian governments opened the dam of opinions and criticisms, putting the Asian values arguments under severe scrutiny. The first critique was focused on the overarching claim of these values as Asian without an eye to the immense geographical, religious, and cultural diversity of Asia. It is noted that the values referred to are not so much 'Asian' as they are those most identified with Confucianism, which leaves out Asian countries without a Confucian past. In this sense, then, 'Asian values' is a misnomer.[18] Another criticism was that while arguments for the Asian values claim to protect the culture-specificity of these values, leaders pick and choose from other cultures, adopting what promotes their interest, such as their ready embrace of the capitalist market and consumerism. Human rights, thus, are upheld for expediency and not for their intrinsic value.[19] 'The so-called Asian values that are invoked to justify authoritarianism are not especially Asian in any significant way. Nor is it easy to see how they could be made, by the mere force of rhetoric, into an Asian cause against the West.'[20]

The communitarian argument suffers from at least two weaknesses. One is that it overstates the sharp contrast between the individualism of Western society and the primacy of community in Asian societies.[21] Individualism, I hold, is the blight of us all, just as the value of community is found in the best of all traditions. The second weakness is the easy but wrong assumption that the Asian governments, that is, the States, are the 'community'. The community and State are different institutions and often are in contrary juxtaposition. The community is governed by popular norms enacted by negotiation, persuasion, and consensus; the State, unless it is humanized and democratized, which it has not been in most of Asia, imposes itself on society through draconian laws, military force, and discriminatory sanctions.[22]

The 'liberty trade-off,' claimed to be an Asian approach to human rights, given its peculiar socio-economic reality, is ethically flawed and politically falsifying. It creates a false dilemma. The truth is that an authoritarian regime, without the pressure of free press and the freedom of speech and assembly, can without impunity both repress and starve its people.[23] 'The leaders who are in a position to encroach upon citizens' rights to express political opinions will also be beyond reproach and accountability for failures to protect citizens' socio-economic rights.'[24] An end to oppression often means the alleviation of poverty. Amartya Sen points out that 'no substantial famine has ever occurred in any independent and democratic country with a relatively free press.'[25] One sees, thus, that all human rights are universal, indivisible, and interdependent.

> Civil and political rights can fuel social and economic growth. The exercise of civil and political freedom, the right to vote and freedom of speech calls governments to attend to real economic needs . . . The right of political participation fortifies the government's public mandate to continue to work for greater prosperity. Civil and political rights and economic and social rights reinforce one another and together ensure greater respect for human dignity and well-being.[26]

The Asian values debate is a discourse on the relation of culture specificity and universality of human rights. Human rights doctrine and language take shape in the cultural, economic, and political history of a people – the terrain where their battles for a just and humane society are fought. But there are core human values that bind us all, transcending our political histories and cultural peculiarities. The adoption of the Universal Declaration of Human Rights in 1948 and of the United Nations Millennium Goals of 2000 attest to the reality of an interdependent world, where we all are bound by a common moral order, in which we find a final recourse.

This balance between culture specificity and the universality of human rights is witnessed in the evolving shape of the Philippine Bill of Rights over the years, representing the turns of the history of the Filipino people, which climaxed in the revolution of 1986. Leaving their distinctive mark on their laws and rights, the Filipinos never lost their sense of national identity. The following was written in 1920: 'Notwithstanding the long Spanish dominion over the Philippines, and notwithstanding the shorter, although more influential American control, native traditions and customs, in their essentials, have remained unaffected. Outward form has changed, but inward thought has not changed. The Filipino has neither been transmuted into a Spaniard nor an American. What we might term the Filipino soul has survived the centuries of contact with foreign races.'[27] But when the Bill of Rights of 1973 forged by the Marcos dictatorship did not prevent it from committing human rights violations, the International Bill of Human Rights was invoked to take action against those violations and the dictatorship itself. The Universal Declaration that 'human rights should be protected . . . if man is not to be compelled to have recourse, as a last resort, to rebellion against tyranny and oppression,' rendered the 1986 People Power Revolution a legitimate uprising of a people for their fundamental human rights.[28]

Here we see the need for both culture specificity and universality. Thus, we do not go to the extreme of cultural relativism resulting in ethnocentric blindness[29] or the extreme of universalism resulting in mindless hegemony. What we aim at is a culturally-inclusive universalism, where universal human values find valency and legitimacy in cultures and cultural values are grounded in inherent universal human rights. For culturally-inclusive universalism to be achieved, there must be a continuing cross-cultural conversation and education at the level of both theory and practice.[30] This takes the view that 'human rights cannot go truly global unless it goes deeply local.'[31] As the philosopher Martha Naussbaum observes, 'there are features of humanness that lie beneath all local traditions and are there to be seen whether or not they are in fact recognized in local traditions.'[32] The task of continuing cross-cultural conversation and education is to bring these features to greater visibility and recognition.

Concluding Statement

There is a perception that regards human rights as peculiarly Western and claims that Asia has little or nothing to contribute from its own traditions. The growing literature on human rights from an Asian perspective dispels this misconception. Asian scholars and human rights activists have found their place in the global human rights discourse in both thought and practice, enriching it from their unique Asian experience. What may have originated from the West has taken on new forms and language in Asia. But long before, far back in antiquity and throughout history when people fought for their basic human rights as individuals and as a collective, human rights was first a reality before it was a concept.

Notes

1. Jean Porter, *Nature as Reason: A Thomistic Theory of the Natural Law*, Grand Rapids, Michigan: Eerdmans, 2005, p. 343.
2. Brian Tierney, *The Idea of Natural Rights: Studies in Natural Rights, Natural Law, and Church Law, 1150-1625*, Atlanta: Scholars Press, 1997, see pp. 13–77.
3. Porter, *Nature as Reason*, pp. 347–8.
4. Tierney, *Idea of Natural Rights*, p. 54.
5. Porter, *Nature as Reason*, pp. 350–1.
6. See *Ibid.*, pp. 358–77, for Porter's discussion.
7. Xiarong Li, '"Asian Values" and the Universality of Human Rights', http://www.puaf.umd.edu/IPPP/li.htm, accessed 17 July 2009, 1-7, here at 7.
8. Yash Ghai, 'The Asian Perspective on Human Rights', http://www.hrsolidarity.net/mainfile.php/1993vol05no03/2061/, accessed 17 July 2009, 1-5, here at 1.
9. David Hollenbach, S.J., called this pursuit of shared vision of the good life intellectual solidarity. 'It is an intellectual endeavour, for it calls for serious thinking by citizens about what their distinctive understandings of the good imply for a life of a society made up of people with many different traditions.' *The Common Good and Christian Ethics*, Cambridge: Cambridge University Press, 2002, pp. 137–8).
10. Porter, *Nature as Reason*, p. 378. In view of the providential role that moral diversity plays, Porter takes a contrary position to that of Lisa Cahill, who affirms the ideal of a universal common good. See Cahill, 'Toward Global Ethics', *Theological Studies* 63 (2002), 324–44.
11. Annette Baier, 'Claims, Rights, Responsibilities', in *Prospects for a Common Morality*, ed. Gene Outka & John Reeder, Jr., Princeton: Princeton University Press, 1993, pp. 149–69, here at 152.
12. Porter, *Nature as Reason*, pp. 359–60.
13. *Ibid.*
14. Randall Peerenboom, 'Human Rights and Asian Values: The Limits of Universalism', *China Review International*, vol. 7, no. 2, 295–320, here at 295–6. Also see Daniel A. Bell, 'The East Asian Challenge to Human Rights: Reflection on an East-West Dialogue', *Human Rights Quarterly* 18.3 (1996), 641–67.
15. Cited in Chai, 'The Asian Perspective on Human Rights', 2.
16. Joanne Bauer, 'The Challenge to International Rights', http://www.cceia.org/resources/articles papers reports/905.html, accessed 17 July 2009, 1–9, here

at 3. See also Hurights Osaka, 'Human Rights and the "Asian" Perspective', http://www.hurights.or.jp/asia-pacific/no_10/no10_asian.htm, accessed 17 July 2009, 1–5.

17. Singapore Institute of International Affairs, 'What are Human Rights? The Nature and Source of Human Rights', http://www.siiaonline.org/ ?==programmes/commentary/what-are-human-rights-the-nature-. . . accessed 17 July 2009, 1–8, here at 5–6.

18. Bauer, 'The Challenge to International Rights', 3.

19. Li, '"Asian Values" and the Universality of Human Rights', 2.

20. Amartya Sen, 'Human Rights and Asian Values', *The New Republic*, July 14–21, 1997, in http://www.mtholyoke.edu/acad/intrel/sen.htm, accessed 7/17/2009, 1–11, here at 10.

21. Ghai, 'The Asian Perspective on Human Rights', 3.

22. *Ibid.*, 3–4.

23. Li, '"Asian Values" and the Universality of Human Rights', 4.

24. *Ibid.*, 5.

25. Sen, 'Human Rights and Asian Values', 2.

26. Singapore Institute of International Affairs, 'What are Human Rights? The Nature and Sources of Human Rights', 6.

27. George A. Malcolm, 'Constitutional History of Philippines' (1920), VI (4), *American Bar Association Journal* 109, 112.

28. See Soliman M. Santos, Jr., 'Of Centenaries and Centennials: A Filipino Contribution to the Australian Debate on a Bill of Rights', *Australian Journal of Human Rights*, at http://www.austlii.edu.au/au/journals/AJHR/2000/8. html, accessed 17 July 2009, 1–30, here at 14.

29. Matthew Weinberg cites Robert Edgerton's work, *Sick Societies Challenging the Myth of Primitive Harmony* (New York: The Free Press, 1992). He writes: 'His research demonstrates that entire societies are sick – a reference to the systematic and unjust treatment of certain of its members such as women – and that such dysfunctional societies inevitably perish [. . .] their social and decision-making structures serve no other purpose than to institutionalize inequality and injustice. Thus, the mere fact that differences across cultures exist does not mean that all variations in social and cultural practices are right or acceptable. On these grounds, relativism itself has been critiqued as immoral.' Matthew Weinberg, 'The Human Rights Discourse: A Bahái Perspective', http://info. bahai.org/article1-8-3-2.html, accessed 17 July 2009, 1–15, here at 3.

30. See Boaventura de Sousa Santos, 'Toward a Multicultural Conception of Human Rights', in Berta Hernández-Truyol (ed.), *Moral Imperialism: A Critical Authority*, New York: New York University Press, 2002); Wolfgang Koener, 'Human Rights: Toward a Common Understanding', http://dsp-psd.pwgsc. gc.ca/collection-R/LoPBdP/BP/bp332-e.htm, accessed 17 July 2009, 1–11.

31. Cited in Elizabeth More, 'The Universal Declaration of Human Rights in

Today's World', http://www.internationalcommunicationsjournal.com/ issues/volume-11-no-2/the-universal-... accessed 17 July 2009, 1–11, here at 1.

32. Cited in Weinberg, 'The Human Rights Discourse: a Baháí Perspective', 4.

Life-centred Ethics, Healing, and Public Health in Africa

JACQUINEAU AZETSOP

Introduction

The concept of 'vital force' that shapes the traditional African understanding of human existence demands an approach to morality which is life- and
community-centred. The meaning of life is essentially given through the
cosmic order. But the social unfolding of the vital force results from social
discussion that takes place in the 'palaver' setting. The vital force can be seen
as an expression of natural law, since it is a force of progress that aims at
improving social cohesion and individual responsibility for the community.
Health is one of those goods whose instrumental value and substantive
nature is recognized in every human society. In traditional African cultures,
the community was a therapeutic-management group because healing was
seen as a communal venture. The goal of this presentation is to show that a
reliance on the African ethics of life fosters an approach to healing, health,
and bioethics that is population-based as well as an approach to natural law
that is essentially relational and not primarily rational.

I. A life-centerd ethics

The most important feature of philosophical anthropology in the African
context is the concept of vital force through which the human person is
understood as a being in relationship. The concept of 'vital force' was first
coined by Placide Tempels,[1] a Franciscan missionary who set out to demonstrate the existence of an ethics and metaphysics proper to the Bantus. Like
Tempels, many African anthropologists and thinkers have used this concept
to convey the fact that life is a force that grows, diminishes, and vanishes in
relation to phases of the human existence. However, to qualify it as philosophical does not mean that it is not real. Life is experienced as belonging,
communion, sharing, hospitality, celebration, and participation. Human

existence is experienced as abundance of life and well-being in its material, spiritual, social, and psychological aspects. In most traditional religions, all principles of morality and ethics are to be sought within the context of preserving human life and its power or force.[2] This same concept of vital life is the main principle of African traditional thinking.[3]

Life is the driving force behind African morality. The cosmic harmony depends on the harmony that exists among beings, a sort of hierarchical ordering of realities.[4] Life appears then as the unifying factor of human existence, for it binds together social forces, members of the community, the living and the dead, born and unborn, and the visible and invisible in such a way that there is no separation between the secular and the religious or the human and the divine.[5] Life is also a key determinant of morality. The morality of an act is determined by its life-giving potential: good acts are those that contribute to the community's vital force, whereas bad acts, however apparently insignificant, are those that tend to diminish life.[6]

II. An ethics of solidarity and personal autonomy: the value of the community

Human existence attains its fulfilment when it is perceived as 'communion-with' and 'participation-in'. The human being cannot just be understood and conceived as an individual, but as a being always caught up in a web of relationships. The Heideggerian project to restore fundamental ontology does not work well in the African context, for a being is not conceived in a solipsistic way, but rather in a communal sense of a being-in-relationship. The knowing and thinking processes are also shaped by this relational anthropology: to know a thing is to grasp the complex set of relationships that define it. In this line of thought, 'human understanding is determined not so much by the Cartesian *Cogito ergo sum* as by *cognatus sumus, ergo sumus*, i.e. by being related'.[7]

Social harmony requires that society consider each of its members as a subject. It has been argued for a long time that the dimension of individuality was alien to African societies,[8] but this thesis has been contradicted by Benezet Bujo and many other African thinkers. Solidarity is not genuine unless it ensures the respect due to each person. Here, the palaver is extremely important because it guarantees the capacity of individuals to provide new experiences that enrich the community.[9] However, the African ethics of life is not a freedom-centred ethics that considers the self-determination of the moral agent to be the goal of decision-making. African morality is not an individualistic morality; it is rather a morality of virtue, responsibility, and commu-nality.[10] By responsibility, I mean a caring attitude or conduct one feels one ought to adopt with respect to the well-being of other persons. Such a caring attitude or conduct includes the responsibility to help others in distress, the responsibility not to harm others, and so on.[11] In an African setting, claiming a right is not prior to responsibility and duty, especially responsibility toward human life and the community. The autonomy of the moral subject is not considered as the end or precondition of the act. Rather the progress of the whole community, which includes the well-being of the individual person, is the main goal. In fact, the moral shaping of the individual reflects the core values of the entire community. However, each member of the community subscribes to these values according to his or her own genius and personality. The community plays an important role in shaping the life of its members. The human person is seen as an intrinsically communal being, embedded in a context of social relationships and interdependence, never as an autono-mous individual. The community cannot be understood as a simple asso-ciation of individuals whose interests and ends are contingently congruent, but as a group of persons linked by interpersonal bonds (biological and/or non-biological) who consider themselves primarily as members of the group and who have common interests, goals and values.[12]

The community is instrumental in the moral growth of the individual person. The inherently relational character of the person and the mutual dependence of human persons arising from the natural communality indi-cate the radical importance of the community in the life of individuals. The individual person is fully complete when he or she is caught up in the web of relationships. The idea of the autonomous, self-sufficient human person arising from the Enlightenment does not work because human finitude and limitedness stress the existential and ontological limits of human autonomy. Our capacities, talents, and dispositions are not adequate for the realization of our potential and basic needs unless we rely on others.[13] The person is not then an autonomous being who derives the rules of moral conduct solely from personal judgment. Since African ethics is a cosmo–ethics, personal behaviour affects the whole cosmos. Therefore, the moral subject cannot avoid reflecting on the manner in which his or her behaviour affects the community. In our contemporary era, people have become sensitive to the interconnection between social and ecological phenomena.

Disease causation and healing

The communal dimension of human existence also influences the African conception of healing and illness. Healing is not just limited to the patient-physician relationship, but rather involves the entire community because the community or clan is a therapeutic management group. An illness starts with a subjective perception of its effects, until the community recognizes it and allows the sick person to play the role of one afflicted by disease.[14] The social dimension of the disease is underlined by the fact that the disease is perceived not just as a biological problem but also as a result of an imbalance in the cosmic order. The disharmony that leads to the disease gives the individual and the community the opportunity to evaluate their relationships inside and outside the community. The clan or the family is involved in the healing process from the initial identification of the disease to the final process of healing. Healing involves rituals, sacrifices, offerings, a process of reconciliation, and remedies such as potions to drink. It also includes the physical, emotional, psychological, spiritual, and communal dimension of the person. The purpose of all these symbolic and curative actions is to restore the initial power of life. Traditional African healing offers instruction regarding the ways the community can help in healthcare. It teaches that the human body is part of a larger ecology characterized by its interconnectedness. An important goal in such a communal setting is the preservation of the cosmic harmony by a constant communion at all the levels of human life.

Traditional healing focused both on the well-being of the community and the health of sick persons. The understanding was that it is only within the community of care and love that true healing is possible. On the other hand, health was seen as an important value that made other values possible and achievable. As long as one was healthy little else mattered and all other achievements were within the bounds of the possible. Health care within traditional Africa was within the reach of all, no matter one's social status, because being ill was the only condition for access to health care.[15] Western medicine is undoubtedly more structured than African medicine. However, Western medicine seems to have fallen into the trap of profit-seeking companies. Morally blind market integrists who rule the market economy have usurped medicine to the extent that ethical and medical issues are discussed primarily in economic terms. While the African conception of health and healing does not differentiate health from other aspects of well-being, it does not allow for the possibility that (some) well-being might be achieved while health is bad, or that health might be good yet well-being low. The African conception of health and healing questions the biomedical understanding of healing through which 'the treatment for diseases . . . is to be accomplished on an individual basis, and through bio-chemo-surgical processes. The social causes of illness and their relevance and implications, are relegated to a category of secondary importance.'[16] That is why 'It would be ideal to combine the efficiency of Western science and technology with the moral sensibilities of traditional Africa. Western culture could empower African culture while African culture humanized Western culture'.[17]

Disease causation and model of illness explanation

The concept of vital force and the relational understanding of the human person that it promotes are adequate to the challenge of providing the foundation for a given model of disease explanation, as well as an approach to bioethics that transcends the biomedical framework. Because each person is inherently social and because society is supposed to be a life-protecting environment, theories of disease causation and the 'ethics of the living' cannot ignore the cultural background and social conditions within which human beings live.

The African explanation of disease is based on the concept that illness is a disturbance of right relationships. Disease 'is not looking at a bad body inside an otherwise healthy body. *Clostridium dificile colitis* is not a bad body one sees under a microscope. The disease is not identical with the bacterium. The disease is a disturbance in the relationships that ought to prevail within the colon of a human being.'[18] Hence, healing is not just about the restoration of physical functioning of the individual but also the restoration of right relationships. It also entails the restoration of social harmony because the body of society can increase vulnerability to pathogens. Social inequities and the lack of social support can play an important role in disease promotion. Social inequities increase vulnerability to pathogens and social support is important for recovery and even for disease prevention. That is why healing cannot be limited to restoration of homeostatic relationships of the individual patient as an isolated organism.[19] The American physician and bioethicist Daniel Sulmasy writes that 'illness disturbs more than relationships inside the human organism. It also disrupts families and workplaces. It shatters pre-existing patterns of coping. It raises questions about one's relationship with the transcendent.'[20]

Holistic healing requires that attention be paid to all aspect of human life. Even when physical and physiological healing is no longer possible, healing is still possible if other aspects of human existence are taken into account. In traditional Africa, a dying person will restore all the broken relationships with others, God, the ancestors, and all the cosmic forces prior to his or her death. Healing can focus on the relationship between the individual person and his or her social environment. Reconciliation, genuine expressions of care and love can bring social and spiritual healing to the dying person. This approach to healing is not understandable within a model of illness explanation that focuses essentially on the restoration of the homeopathic relationships of the patient. It challenges the biological individualism of contemporary bio-medicine. An individualistic conception of health and healing simply places medicine and healthcare under the control of the forces of the market, as is the case in the USA and some other developed countries. Based on the potential of biomedicine and on the moral compass of the ethics of life, I argue for a model of disease explanation and of health care that is holistic. It is a bio-psychological-spiritual model that is not a mere dualism in which a soul accidentally inhabits a body.[21] It is a model in which, 'the biological, psy-chological, social, and spiritual are distinct dimensions of the person, and no individual aspect can be disaggregated from the whole.'[22] This model takes into account the biological, psychological, and spiritual needs of the sick members of the community. It also has a social dimension through which the environment within which disease occurs can be studied and the politi-cal economy of poor health understood. Adopting a sociological model of disease explanation allows us to keep alive the suspicion that social inequities are important contributing factors for poor health at the population level.

III. Significance for population health and implications for bioethics

Through its adoption of the biomedical model of disease that promotes medical individualism and its reliance on an individual-based anthropology, mainstream bioethics has focused predominantly on respect for autonomy in the clinical setting and respect for the person in the research site, emphasiz-ing self-determination and freedom of choice. However, the emphasis on the individual has often led to moral vacuum, exaggeration of human agency, and a thin (liberal?) conception of justice. With such a limited conception of justice, bioethics cannot adequately address collective macro-problems including social, sanitary, and environmental problems that mark everyday life in poor countries. Autonomy-based bioethics fails to engage the lived worlds of diversely constituted and situated social groups, particularly those that are marginalized.[23] Similarly, in clinical medicine, broad issues such as the common good, distributive justice, and the spirituality of the patient can be ignored for the sake of the primacy of secular business concerns.[24] Applied to resource-poor countries and communities within developed countries, autonomy-based bioethics fails to address the root causes of diseases and public health crises with which individuals or communities are confronted. An autonomy-centered ethics places the burden of prevention and access to healthcare on the moral agent. In doing so, it frames disease within a model that limits political intervention in the health domain strictly to biomedical solutions or behaviour change. This leads to the perpetuation of the social *status quo* within which risks for poor health are greater and lends legitimacy to the social forces that increase health risks. Since disease is a social process, a policy vision that focuses on individual risk factors fails to promote social justice and to address structural elements that create conditions favourable to disease. Hence, we need to move from health-care policy to health policy, or rather, a health-care policy that is responsive to facts explaining why (certain) people with (certain) diseases from (certain) communities require medical care. Health policy should embrace healthcare policies but include considerations regarding welfare, work, occupational, economic development, employment, and educational policies. A holistic model of explanation of illness causation is needed to broaden principles of biomedical ethics and provide a renewed understanding of disease, freedom, medical practice, patient-physician relationship, risk and benefit of research and treatment, research priorities, and health policy.

Bioethics scholarship that focuses on the holistic model considers local as well as global issues of social inequality, because this model is premised on the intimate connection that exists between social inequality and health inequality. The distribution of illness is likely to reflect the geography of inequality. A social approach to bioethics emphasizes distributive justice and benefits at both the population and individual level.

IV. Natural law thinking, health, and bioethics

The intimate connection that exists between the cosmic order and the moral order in African culture(s) does not allow an objectifying concept of nature. Doing good and working to maintain social harmony and environmental balance are identical. Human behaviour maintains or disrupts the harmony of the cosmos while the hierarchical structuring of forces indicates where the ultimate values lie. Thus any ethical reflection on health and healing ought to be a cosmo–ethical reflection because every single piece of existence possesses its own dignity, destiny, and sovereignty. Every piece of existence is in itself the cosmos in the making, a microcosm. Therefore, acting well means to behave in such a way that the essentials become concretized in the ordinary life of society. Doing good simply means improving the welfare of the community and increasing the quality of life of people. The cosmic order is an order of life which is expressed through the moral order shaped by rules of conduct and patterns of behaviour set by society after a careful and consensual discussion called palaver. Even though the harmony of the cosmos is a given, its concrete expression in society is shaped by historical circumstances and challenges that individuals faced at a particular time of their history. Reason is surely part of the thinking process through which the meanings of life and health are constantly rethought and reconstructed in the light of the vital force, but the improvement of social relationships is the foundational principle that guides this communication process. Contrary to an exclusively rational conception of natural law, here, the order of nature is essentially relational. The moral standards that govern human behaviour are, in some sense, objectively discovered through a communication process. They are realized subjectively by living to the full the societal laws that emerge from palaver. Even though the palaver is inclusive, influential individuals or groups can control the communication process and impose their views on others. In theory, everyone's view and interests are taken into account, but vulnerable groups such as women and the young can be marginalized.

The relationship between the vital force, which comes from the Supreme Being (God), and the rules and laws that guide life in society cannot be understood purely or primarily as an exclusively rational process but essentially needs to be perceived from the intrinsically relational understanding of human existence. The methodology is not abstract and deductive but communicational and dialogical. The rules of conduct are certainly inspired by the vital force, but ultimately they are set by society's members. Hence, natural law, this organizing principle of life, can only be understood from the relational context that shapes human existence and calls for social progress. Similarly, health needs and challenges as well as the responses given to them cannot be understood from the same context. As the principle of social harmony and life, the concept of vital force impels us to think about health care, health promotion and health justice not only in individual terms but also in population-based terms. Similarly, health needs cannot be understood solely from an individualistic point of view but also from a population-based approach. Thus, the creation of social arrangements and a political environment conducive to good health and well-being is as important as providing access to care.

Conclusion

In most African cultures, the preservation of life and the promotion of social harmony are the main criteria of morality. African ethics is a life- and community-centred morality. As an organizing principle of human existence, the vital force promotes a conception of health and healing which is holistic and population-based. This conception of health and healing is based on the history and needs of people. Similarly, any bioethics reflection that relies on the African approach to human existence must question the use of the biomedical model of illness explanation and must embrace a holistic and a population-based approach to health and ethical principles.

Notes

1. Placide Tempels, *La Philosophie Bantoue*, Paris: Présence Africaine, 1949.
2. Laurenti Magesa. *African Religion: The Moral Traditions of Abundant Life*, Nairobi: Paulines Publication Africa.Laurenti Magesa, 1998, pp 31–2.
3. Martin Nkafu, *African Vitalogy, A Step Forward in African Thinking*, Nairobi: Paulines Publications Africa, 1999, p. 31.
4. Bénézet Bujo, *African Christian Morality at the Age of Inculturation*, Nairobi: Paulines Publications Africa, 1998, p. 20.
5. Magesa, *op. cit.*, p. 72.
6. Benezet Bujo, *African Theology in its Social Context*, Nairobi: Paulines Publications Africa, 1992, p. 26.
7. J. Ilunga-Muya, 'Bénézet Bujo, *The Awakening of a Systematic and Authentically African Thought*', in Bujo and J. Ilungo-Muya (eds), *African Theology: The Contribution of the Pioneers*, Nairobi: Paulines Publications Africa, 2003, p. 125.
8. Bénézet Bujo, *Foundations of an African Ethic: Beyond the Universal Claims of Western Morality*, New York: Herder & Herder, 2001, p. 6.
9. Ilunga-Muya, *op. cit*, 131.
10. Kwame Gyekye, *African Cultural Values: An Introduction*, Philadelphia/Accra: Sankofa Publishing Company, 1996. p. 63.
11. *Ibid.*
12. Kwame Gyekye, 'Person and Community', in K. Gyeke and K. Wiredu (eds), *Cultural Heritage and Contemporary Change*, Washington, DC: CIPSH/UNESCO, 1998, p. 104.
13. *Ibid.*, p. 105.

14. Meinrad Pierre Hebga, *Witchcraft, Sorcery and Illness in Africa*, Nairobi: Hekima College, 1987, p. 4.
15. Godfrey Tangwa, 'The Traditional African Perception of a Person: Some Implications for Bioethics', *Hasting Center Report* 30, 5 (2000), 43.
16. José Lavastida, *Health Care and the Common Good: A Catholic Theory of Justice*, Washington, DC: University Press of America, 2000, p. 87.
17. Godfrey Tangwa, *op. cit*, p. 43.
18. Daniel P. Sulmasy, *The Rebirth of the Clinic: An Introduction to Spirituality in Health Care*, Washington, DC: Georgetown University Press, 2007), p. 125.
19. *Ibid.*
20. *Ibid.*, p. 125.
21. *Ibid.*, p. 128.
22. *Ibid.*
23. Susan Kelly, 'Bioethics and Rural Health: Theorizing Place, Space, and Subjects', *Soc Sci Med* 56 (2003), 2277–88.
24. Richard McCormick, 'Bioethics, a Moral Vacuum', *America* 180 (1999), 21–5.

Bibliography

Bujo, B. *African Christian Morality at the Age of Inculturation.* Nairobi: Paulines Publications Africa, 1998.
——. *African Theology in its Social Context.* Nairobi: Paulines Publications Africa, 1992.
——. *Foundations of an African Ethic: Beyond the Universal Claims of Western Morality.* New York: Herder & Herder, 2001.
Gyekye, K. *African Cultural Values: An Introduction.* Philadelphia/Accra: Sankofa Publishing Company, 1996.
Gyekye, K. 'Person and Community'. Gyeke, K. and Wiredu, K., eds. *Cultural Heritage and Contemporary Change.* Washington, DC: CIPSH/UNESCO, 1998, pp. 101–22.
Hebga, M. P. *Witchcraft, Sorcery and Illness in Africa.* Nairobi: Hekima College, 1987.
Lavastida, J, *Health Care and the Common Good: A Catholic Theory of Justice.* Washington, DC: University Press of America, 2000.
Magesa, L. *African Religion: The Moral Traditions of Abundant Life.* Nairobi: Paulines Publication Africa, 1998.
McCormick, R. 'Bioethics, a Moral Vacuum'. *America* 180 (1999), 21–5.
Nkafu, M. *African Vitalogy, A Step Forward in African Thinking.* Nairobi: Paulines Publications Africa, 1999.
Ilunga-Muya, J. 'Bénézet Bujo, *The Awakening of a Systematic and Authentically African Thought*'. Bujo, B. and Ilungo-Muya, J., eds., *African Theology: The*

Contribution of the Pioneers. Nairobi: Paulines Publications Africa, 2003. pp. 107–49.

Sulmasy, D. P. *The Rebirth of the Clinic: An Introduction to Spirituality in Health Care*. Washington, DC: Georgetown University Press, 2007.

Susan Kelly, 'Bioethics and Rural Health: Theorizing Place, Space, and Subjects'. *Soc Sci Med* 56 (2003), 2277–88.

Tangwa, G. 'The Traditional African Perception of a Person: some Implications for Bioethics'. *Hasting Center Report* 30, 5 (2000), 39–43.

Tempels, P. *La Philosophie Bantoue*. Paris: Présence Africaine, 1949.

Part Two: Theological Forum

The Search for a Universal Ethic: The International Theological Commission's 2009 Document on Natural Law

ANDREA VICINI

The many ethical issues we face today – from ecology to biotechnology – call for our personal and social responsibility in promoting global solidarity. Rights, values, virtues, principles are the ethical resources available, but the emphasis given to each one of them changes greatly, often making dialogue and engagement difficult. A cross-cultural ethical approach grounded in our common humanity could promote interaction and commitment.

In June 2009, the prestigious International Theological Commission (ITC)[1] published the document *The Search for a Universal Ethic: A New Look at Natural Law*[2] to indicate how a renewed understanding of natural law could provide the needed common ethical ground.[3] As far as I can see, this document has so far received very limited attention in theological debates, despite its interest and importance. These pages aim first at presenting the document and then at discussing the choices made by the Commission.

I. An overview

In its five chapters, the ITC focuses on context (I) and human experience (II), develops a theoretical foundation (III), considers the importance of natural law in addressing social and political issues (IV), and examines the relation between reason and faith (V).

The urgency of finding shared values opens the document. These values are already lived by many persons striving to promote 'peace, a more just political order, the sense of a shared responsibility, an equitable share of our wealth, the respect for the environment, the dignity of the human person, and one's fundamental rights' (2).[4] To succeed, we need 'a valid basic agreement on the goods and values that express the deepest human aspirations, personally and communally' (2) and a continuing 'experience of conversion' (4). The ITC appreciates the attempts aimed at promoting 'a common ethical language' (3) – i.e., the *Universal Declaration of Human Rights* (5, 115) and the proposals for a world ethic (6) – and it criticizes the 'juridical positivism that refuses to rely on an objective ontological criterion of what is just' (7) and 'an ethic of discussion' (8) that appears solely procedural.

In searching for a universal ethic, the natural law shows a major advantage: it is our reason that, despite diverse backgrounds, makes us recognize certain fundamental natural ethical orientations in our actions and express them normatively in specific precepts (cf. 9). Because they are rooted in human nature, these inclinations are fundamental, objective, and universal. They promote human dignity and criticize any ideological threat to persons and communities.

The attention given to human experience and social contexts in the Introduction continues in the first chapter, 'Convergences'. The general inclinations that characterize natural law are neither specifically nor exclusively Christian. They can be traced in world religions and wisdom traditions.[5] Furthermore, a historic overview of natural law provides elements for its understanding. In the Greek tragedies, as in Plato, Aristotle, and the Roman Stoics, what belongs to natural law comes before any civil law, and it is at the core of any law (cf. 18–21).

In the early Christian tradition, chosen biblical texts – the covenant with Noah, Wisdom literature, the golden rule of the Gospels, and Paul's emphasis on the unwritten law in every heart (cf. 22–25) – focused on what we share in common. Later, Thomas Aquinas and the Scholastics articulated a compact understanding of the relationship between faith, nature, and reason (cf. 26). During the Middle Ages, the natural law became a mature doctrine with a metaphysical theological structure (cf. 27). While Francisco de Vitoria made it a universal norm to regulate the relations between States, later Scholasticism emphasized voluntarism, by idealizing a subject free from any influence – natural or transcendent (cf. 28–30).

In the Modern Age, Hobbes viewed the law as dependent only on the authority that promulgated and enforced it, without any relation to the good. Hence, nature and reason stood separated, autonomous. By reaction, the natural law became static, rationalistic, a-historical, disconnected from human experience – a rigidly determined set of rules and norms. The empirical sciences rightly demanded a renewed interpretation of natural law (cf. 33).

The ITC ends its historical overview by indicating that the magisterial teaching proposes the natural law: to ground rights on reason and to promote intercultural interreligious dialogue and peace; to affirm the natural and objective character of the fundamental norms that regulate social and political life; to support what strengthens the society's search for common good; to plead for the objection of conscience or civil disobedience (cf. 35).

The second chapter, 'The Perception of Common Moral Values', articulates a genealogical approach where human relations and the cultural context form our moral conscience and our perception of fundamental moral goods. This leads to a formulation of the general precepts of natural law.[6] Aquinas' first moral principle – do good and avoid evil – qualifies the 'moral good', *i.e.*, what goes beyond the useful and aims at human flourishing (cf. 39). Hence, reason helps in discerning the particular goods that contribute to human flourishing (cf. 41) and promotes dialogue among cultures and religions (cf. 42). The natural law promotes our understanding of moral obligation not as if it were exterior to the person ('pure heteronomy') but as fully inseparable from the person (it 'comes from the heart').[7] As a consequence, the perception of moral goods is immediate. By following Aquinas, the ITC indicates that this perception is articulated in the three 'natural dynamisms' that constitute the natural law (cf. 46).

They are: first, 'the inclination to conserve and to develop one's existence', in the case of each substance; second, 'the inclination to reproduce in order to perpetuate the species', in the case of all living creatures; third, 'the inclination to know the truth about God and to live in society', in the case of all human beings (46).[8] The overall moral goal is to live a fully meaningful relational life and to build just social dynamics and structures. These general precepts are considered universal and immutable because they can be recognized in our nature (cf. 52). Because of individual sinfulness and cultural influences, we should be 'modest and prudent' in affirming their evidence, but we should use them to promote dialogue.[9] Caution is also due because we need to articulate and to apply these precepts differently in varying cultures and times (cf. 47, 53–4).

Discernment is required from all moral agents, moralists or not,[10] by asking everyone to keep the tension between the basic precepts of natural law and what concerns the particular concrete precepts (cf. 56). The formation of conscience, discernment, and decision-making (cf. 59) requires a growth in wisdom, a strengthening of the will, and a moral life shaped by 'emotional intelligence' (57) and by the virtues, particularly prudence (cf. 56, 58).

The third chapter, 'The Foundations of Natural Law', sets out the meta-physical theoretical foundations of natural law and reflects on how human nature may be considered morally normative. It offers an explanatory frame-work to ground and to legitimate moral values. The philosophical justifica-tion of natural law is given both on anthropological grounds (some virtuous behaviours promote human and social flourishing more than others) and on a metaphysical basis. Our human dynamism comprehends what we expe-rience about our beginning (we are creatures) and what we aim at as our end (what we strive for by nature). This dynamism is transcendent (it comes from God), but it is also immanent (it is part of who we are).[11] Hence, the subject's ontological specific identity is 'the internal principle of movement that orients the subject toward one's own realization' (64). Nature – which includes the spiritual realm – is the 'real dynamic principle of the subject's development and of the subject's activities' (64). The social fabric results from interactions and relationships among each ontological identity (cf. 65). To this vision, Christianity adds the dimension of freedom, which is essen-tial to understanding ourselves as creatures and persons (cf. 66–7).

As a result, natural law presupposes harmony and participation among God, the person, and nature (cf. 69–70) and orientates us to flourish (cf. 70) and to act, without falling into naturalistic fallacy (cf. 73).

The fourth chapter, 'Natural Law and the City', shows how the natural law is relevant in reflecting on social and political issues, while defining and pursuing the common good (cf. 85). Because of our social nature, the natural law is 'the normative horizon within which the political order should move' (86), and it allows us to identify all the values that make us more humane – liberty, truth, justice, solidarity (cf. 87). Hence, society 'should promote the realization of all personal natural inclinations' (86).[12] Finally, the ITC reminds us to distinguish between political and supernatural order, while preserving the laicity of the State (cf. 96–100).

The fifth chapter, 'Jesus Christ, Fulfilment of Natural Law', outlines the relation between reason and Christian faith. While the natural law express-es the richness of reason, faith enriches reason through grace (cf. 101). In particular, Jesus 'manifests in his person an exemplary human life, fully con-formed to natural law. He is the definitive criterion for correctly deciphering what authentic natural human desires are' (105). Because 'The new law of the gospel includes, assumes, and fulfils the exigencies of natural law' (112), in living by the gospel we fully develop our humanity, dialogue, and search for the common good (cf. 112).

II. Some comments

In today's globalized world, ethical issues need specific solutions but can also benefit from a consistent and coherent ethical framework focused on human dignity and the common good. The ITC believes in an open-ended search for a universal ethic rooted in a shared understanding of human nature, and it proposes an interpretation of the natural law as its ethical foundation. As in Aquinas, the natural law is not understood as a static pre-determined set of norms and rules, but as a dynamic theory, which progressively integrates all that is human (cf. 114), and which sees God, creation, and human persons as dynamically related (cf. 70, 113).[13]

The ITC chooses an inductive approach, by turning to human experience, to anthropological reflection, and to contributions that come from different cultures, philosophies, religions, and wisdom traditions. This hermeneutical methodology promotes dialogue.[14] A metaphysical foundation is considered important to give an account of our essence as human beings (cf. 113). The risk of a biological understanding of the human essence is avoided by considering human nature as a theological concept, and by proposing a relational ontology that focuses on our social nature and finds our spiritual and material unity in human reason (cf. 72). However, any metaphysical foundation presupposes a vision of the good to be pursued – agreeing on which is a challenge in our multi-cultural, fragmented, post-modern world (cf. 2). In the ITC document, due attention is given to magisterial teaching, the Church Fathers, and medieval authors: I would have appreciated an explicit debate with contemporary international contributors to the study of natural law, but this is not the ITC's style.[15]

A further choice made by the ITC is to focus its critical analysis on society and politics.[16] While these are important areas, the natural law is also used extensively in magisterial teaching on human life,[17] love,[18] sexuality,[19] procreation, and, generally, on bioethical issues. These domains could have benefited from critical analysis by the ITC.

For instance, the Commission could have clarified how reflection on basic human inclinations leads us to articulate norms and principles for decision-making, paying attention to the hermeneutical relevance of social context and human experience, as well as to the theoretical implications of a relational ontology. It could have addressed the tension between the teleological purpose of natural law – personal and social flourishing – and the deontological aspect, which concerns specific norms that need to be formulated personally, historically, and socially. For example, there is an ongoing debate about how to move from basic values and goals to specific norms in bioethical matters.

The Commission affirms an objective universal ethic and differentiates basic universal claims, which are unchangeable because rooted in our nature, from more specific ethical norms, which are culturally generated and changeable. This provokes the question of how the ITC views this distinction in the concrete. What is the relevance of experience, history, and culture to the judgments of our practical reason and to moral action within the variability, uncertainty, and indeterminacy of human life and history (cf. 53–54)?

Finally, the document would be strengthened by an explanation of what is 'objective' in the case of values, the good, the truth, and specific ethical precepts (cf. 1, 5, 7–10, 29, 35, 59, 72, 80, 92). This would be particularly helpful while searching for a universal ethic within contemporary cultural, social, and philosophical contexts that challenge the mere possibility of affirming something 'objective' for everyone and everywhere.

With the ITC, we can conclude by inviting all experts within religions and wisdom traditions (and, I add, all people of good will), to continue searching for a universal ethic. First, all must reflect on the relevant sources in their own traditions. Then, in a spirit of mutually respectful criticism, all can work to express 'the fundamental values for our common humanity, in order to work together to promote understanding, reciprocal recognition, and pacific cooperation among all the components of the human family' (116).

Notes

1. See http://www.vatican.va/roman_curia/congregations/cfaith/cti_documents/ rc_con_cfaith_pro_14071997_ictheology_it.html (last accessed 6 Oct. 2009).
2. See http://www.vatican.va/roman_curia/congregations/cfaith/cti_index.htm (last accessed 31 Oct. 2009). The document is about 50 printed pages long (116 numbered paragraphs). It is currently available only in Italian and in French. Some of the bibliographic references, a few mistakes in translation, and missing words in the Italian version, indicate that it was originally written in French.
3. The document was prepared by an *ad hoc* sub-commission. It was discussed during the ITC's plenary sessions in 2006, 2007, and 2008 (when it was unanimously approved).
4. I refer to the document's paragraph numbers. The translations are mine.
5. They are: Hinduism (13), Buddhism (14), Taoism and Confucianism (15), African traditions (16), and Islam (17).
6. These precepts 'are not a complete code of untouchable prescriptions, but a permanent and normative principle that is a source of inspiration at the service of the person's concrete moral life' (11).
7. 43.

8. See also 48–50 and *Summa Theologiae*, I–II, q. 94, a. 2.

9. Those who want to promote dialogue 'should learn to set aside their particular interests in order to open themselves to others' needs and to be challenged by common moral values' (52).

10. 'The moralist [. . .] should use the combined resources of theology and philosophy, as well as human sciences, economics, and biology to recognize clearly the facts of the situation and to identify correctly the concrete demands of human dignity' (54).

11. Cf. 63.

12. On natural law, natural rights, and positive rights, see 88–92.

13. The natural law 'is not a list of definitive and immutable precepts. It is a source of inspiration that always gushes in searching for an objective foundation of a universal ethic' (113).

14. For Christians, Christ reveals the fullness of being human by realizing it in his person, 'But this revelation confirms elements that are already present in the rational thought of humanity's wisdoms' (114).

15. An exception is Hans Küng, *Global Responsibility: In Search of a New World Ethic* (New York: Continuum, 1996). See footnote 5.

16. The ITC also briefly addresses ecology (cf. 1, 81–2).

17. An exception is: '[. . .] deliberate and willed suicide goes against the natural inclination to preserve and fructify one's existence'. (80)

18. '[. . .] the high spiritual value that is expressed by one's gift of self in the context of the spouses' mutual love is already written in the nature of the sexed body, that finds in this spiritual fulfilment its ultimate meaning (*raison d'être*)' (79).

19. Cf. 34. Sexual behaviours are sins against nature 'insofar as they contradict more directly the objective meaning of natural dynamism that persons needs to integrate in the unity of their moral life' (81). Further, 'The moral evaluation of sins against nature must consider not only their objective gravity, but also the objective dispositions, often mitigating, of those who commit them' (n. 76). Then, 'some sexual practices are directly opposed to the reproductive finalities written in the person's sexual body. Hence, they also contradict the interpersonal values that should promote a sexual responsible and fully human life' (80). After its critique of any dualist approach (cf. 74), the ITC adds that 'The ideology of gender, which denies any anthropologic and moral meaning to natural sexual difference between the sexes, belongs to (*s'inscrit dans*) this dualist perspective' (n. 72).

Torture as an Attack on the Human

KENNETH HIMES

There is a great deal of formal opposition to torture around the world. Despite torture's presence throughout history and continuation in the present era, the condemnation of torture is near universal and absolute. For example, the Convention Against Torture and Other Cruel, Inhuman or Degrading Treatment (CIDT) or Punishment states clearly that 'No exceptional circumstance whatsoever, whether a state of war or a threat of war, internal political instability, or any other public emergency may be invoked as a justification for torture'.[1]

Noteworthy about the condemnations of torture and CIDT is that they are stronger and more absolute than opposition to killing. Many who vigorously oppose any exception to the ban on torture are willing to allow the direct killing of another human being. What is it about torture that leads many people to seek an absolute ban on it? Because of the scandals associated with U.S. treatment of detainees during the Presidency of George W. Bush, this essay will focus on the work of recent American authors who have examined the basis for moral opposition to torture.

I. Why is torture wrong?

The theologian Sumner Twiss presents a three-part argument for the absolute wrongfulness of torture. Examining the history of debate preceding the UN Universal Declaration of Human Rights, including the prohibition of torture, he suggests that certain claims about human rights involve 'practical moral apprehensions' that are 'shared by people belonging to diverse, even somewhat antagonistic, moral traditions'.[2] In this Twiss adopts the moral intuitions of Jacques Maritain, who was influential in the UN debates.

The second argument Twiss employs is what he calls a 'minimal natural law position': that is, a 'minimal vision of the human good' that is 'shorn of religious implications'. This minimalist natural law 'implies the claim that human beings share significant common characteristics in virtue of which some conditions and practices are bad for every human being and some other conditions and practices are good for every human being'.[3] Here Twiss echoes the position of the legal theorist Michael Perry.[4]

Finally, Twiss makes consequentalist arguments to establish the wrong-fulness of torture. He suggests that torture inevitably brings about negative consequences not only to the victim, but also to 'persons and communities other than the primary victim'. His argument involves empirically based hypotheses 'about the metastatic tendency or uncontrollability of the admin-istration of torture'.[5] These three approaches to the issue of torture, accord-ing to Twiss, demonstrate that there exists an 'overlapping consensus on the absolute proscription of torture' and that there may even be an overlapping consensus on the rationale for that judgment.[6]

The philosopher David Sussman observes that, since Cesare Beccaria's *On Crime and Punishment* of 1764, 'there has developed a broad and con-fident consensus that torture is uniquely "barbaric" and "inhuman".'[7] He argues the reason for this is that torture at its core is 'a distinctive kind of wrong that is not characteristically found in other forms of extreme violence or coercion'.[8]

The shape of Sussman's argument is Kantian, but he does not limit his claim of torture's wrongfulness simply to the claim that it undermines 'the victim's capacities for rational self-governance'. Rather, he views torture as a practice that 'forces its victim into the position of colluding against him-self through his own affects and emotions' such that the victim is 'actively complicit in his own violation'.[9] At least that is the case with torture for the purpose of interrogation.

For Sussman and other commentators the context of torture is one in which the victim and the torturer(s) are in a 'profoundly asymmetric rela-tionship of dependence and vulnerability'.[10] Victims are completely at the mercy of the torturer, unable to evade or retaliate; victims also realize that the torturer is trying to make them act against their own choices and com-mitments.[11]

Sussman maintains that although the utilitarian and orthodox Kantian arguments against torture can be strong, neither captures the full signifi-cance of torture. Borrowing from the insights of Elaine Scarry, Sussman suggests that 'what the torturer does is to take his victim's pain, and through it his victim's body, and make it begin to express the torturer's will. . . . The victim experiences suffering as not simply something inflicted upon the self but as something the victim does to himself, a kind of self-betrayal worked through my body and feelings.'[12] By resisting the torturer the victim brings about more suffering and pain to his or her body. In that way the victim is not simply passive but turned into 'an active accomplice' in the cruelty.[13] Thus, survivors of torture frequently suffer a 'profound alienation from their own affective and emotional lives'.[14]

Furthermore, it is not simply that the victim eventually *loses* control due to the dominant power of the torturer, it is that the victim experiences the self as *giving up* control. Torture victims share a similarity with rape victims who 'often obsess over the question of whether they resisted enough or whether they let themselves "give in" too readily'.[15]

Law professor David Luban proposes that torture is absolutely wrong for many people because it is particularly offensive to Western liberal beliefs about the relationship of the State to the individual.[16] He argues that 'torture is a microcosm, raised to the highest level of intensity, of the tyrannical political relationships that liberalism hates the most'.[17] In short, Luban's argument against torture is context-dependent, presuming a set of background beliefs associated with the broad liberal tradition that has shaped Western culture.

For Luban, 'torture has always been bound up with military conquest, regal punishment, dictatorial terror, forced confessions, and the repression of dissident belief – a veritable catalogue of the evils of absolutist government that liberalism abhors'.[18] Luban maintains that torture to interrogate a detainee, even one with information about planned terrorist attacks, is yet another tyrannical offence that ought to be anathema to the liberal imagination.

There are clear deontological elements in the arguments of Twiss and Sussman that begin with a conception of the human person and then what is impermissible in the way that persons are to be treated. Luban does not make his case by an explicitly universal appeal, though one may infer that he thinks the liberal understanding of the person is essentially correct and applicable to non-western individuals.

II. A necessary religious argument?

The law professor Jeremy Waldron believes what is needed is 'a clear and unequivocal *framework* in which the issue of torture can be discussed'. He laments that such a framework, once strong and clear in public documents, is now weak and confused owing to the arguments and actions of the Bush administration, whose 'aim was to create an atmosphere of confusion in which honorable people, inside and outside the armed forces, would come to think of the rule against torture as a muddled and difficult technical issue rather than a clear and uncompromising prohibition'.[19]

Waldron wants to see the exception-less ban on torture re-stated and strengthened both in law and the cultural consensus. For this to happen he thinks the Christian theological tradition must 'supplement the rather ashen and impoverished moral vocabulary of secular commentators'. He offers several examples of ethical ideas in the Christian tradition, including the teaching of moral absolutes that would be useful in rebuilding the ethical framework for discussing torture. Further, Waldron maintains that 'a prohibition based on divine command has credentials that transcend' calculations of rationalist utility.[20] In order to be persuasive, Waldron believes, a strong deontological argument requires theological support.

Enter into the conversation the moral theologian Jean Porter of Notre Dame University. She asks, 'What is the status of the norm prohibiting torture? Does it rest on a divine command (and if so, which one), or on some other basis?' According to Porter we cannot claim any direct biblical injunction banning torture and for much of history 'it was not obvious to our Christian forebears that God forbids torture'.[21]

It seems plausible to Porter to maintain that torture violates the fundamental commandment to love one's neighbour. Such an 'analysis moves from a judgment that a particular kind of action comprises an especially egregious violation of human dignity, towards the conclusion that this act violates God's will as expressed through the commandment of neighbour-love'. Note, however, 'the appeal to God's commandment does not add anything by way of justification for the conclusion that torture is an assault on human dignity – the logic of the argument goes in the opposite direction'.[22]

Porter understands the appeal of a divine sanction for moral teaching but observes that the 'distinction between God's law and human *mores* is not as sharp' as Waldron assumes. For 'no matter what we take the starting points of normative reflection to be, whether we ground these in God's law or a natural law or the categorical imperative, these starting points can only become effective as norms through communal processes of reflection and practice' that eventually yield judgments about what counts as right and wrong behaviour.[23] For Porter an absolute ban on torture 'cannot be defended on the basis of its status as a supposed divine command'. Such a 'judgment comes as the conclusion of a normative argument, not as its starting point'.[24]

Porter then takes up the question of what argument can be used to support an absolute prohibition of torture. She states her conviction that torture is an attack on the image of God that each person embodies, yet she admits such a claim is too general to justify an absolute prohibition, given that the image of God within each person does not prevent us from taking the life of the other in extreme circumstances.

Following Thomas Aquinas, Porter alleges that the *imago Dei* in the human person is rooted in the 'human capacities for rational judgment, choice and free action in accordance with that choice'; in other words, rational freedom. Torture is wrong not simply because it is coercive, after all, the experience of being forced to do things we do not wish to do is common. Torture, however, 'subverts the will itself by assaulting or undermining the delicate psychic forces that sustain the individual's integrity, sense of well-being and self-command'.[25]

Porter concludes that torture attacks the capacity of its victims to experience themselves as spiritual creatures. 'No considerations of personal or national security, nor even the possibility of widespread loss of life, can justify an assault' upon 'the integrity of the image of God within the individual, his or her capacities for faith, hope, and love.' That is the 'fundamental theological reason' that torture should be banned absolutely.[26]

Conclusion

This review of contemporary authors reveals they all share the conviction that torture strikes at something inherent in the person that is fundamental. They employ different words to name it, but the common thread running through their arguments is that torture violates the nature of the person in a direct and invidious manner that not even killing does. For that reason, these scholars affirm that torture ought to be banned without exception.

Notes

1. Article 2.2.
2. Sumner Twiss, 'Torture, Justification, and Human Rights: Toward an Absolute Proscription', *Human Rights Quarterly* 29 (2007): 346–367, here 354.
3. *Ibid.*, 356.
4. Perry's argument is found in his essay 'Are Human Rights Universal? The Relativist Challenge and Related Matters', *Human Rights Quarterly* 19 (1997): 461–509.
5. Twiss, 'Torture, Justification, and Human Rights', 358.
6. *Ibid.*, 364–5.

7. David Sussman, 'What's Wrong with Torture?', *Philosophy and Public Affairs* 33/1 (2005) 1–33, here 2.
8. *Ibid.*, 3.
9. *Ibid.*, 4.
10. *Ibid.*, 6
11. *Ibid.*, 10.
12. *Ibid.*, 21. The reference to Scarry is the now classic, *The Body in Pain* (New York: Oxford University Press, 1985.) Chapter one is devoted to her analysis of torture.
13. *Ibid.*, 23.
14. *Ibid.*, 24, n. 33.
15. *Ibid.*, 28.
16. David Luban, 'Liberalism, Torture, and the Ticking Bomb', *Virginia Law Review* 91 (2005): 1425–61.
17. *Ibid.*, 1430.
18. *Ibid.*, 1438.
19. Jeremy Waldron, 'What Can Christian Teaching Add to the Debate about Torture?', *Theology Today* 63 (2006): 330–43, here 335.
20. *Ibid.*, 337.
21. 'Torture and the Christian Conscience: a response to Jeremy Waldron'. *Scottish Journal of Theology* 61/3 (2008): 340–58, here 343.
22. *Ibid.*, 343.
23. *Ibid.*, 344.
24. *Ibid.*, 345.
25. *Ibid.*, 349.
26. *Ibid.*, 351.

A Look at the Concept of Human Nature

IVONE GEBARA

Whenever we speak of human nature we are, almost against our will, led to believe that 'something' exists, a more or less fixed or immutable content to which we ascribe this concept. We often hear phrases such as, 'That's only natural', 'That goes against nature', 'natural beings', 'sins against nature', and so on.

Ultimately, what are we referring to when we speak of 'nature'? What is nature? Who is nature? How do we determine the nature of beings? Is culture perhaps opposed to nature?

I shall not be able, here, to survey the concept of nature in the history of philosophy and theology, let alone in that of the biological sciences. I propose to develop three brief points as a contribution to an ancient and extensive subject, one that continues to permeate all ecological thinking in the twenty-first century.

I. Nature as divine creature

In the patriarchal Christian tradition, the myth of creation gave rise to the idea that God creates *ex nihilo*. 'Nothing' is an empty concept that, in effect, indicates the divine creative power with no mediation whatever. In this sense, 'nothing' is an imaginary concept, especially when it relates to the absence of any material element. We can say, 'There is nothing in this box', to indicate an absence of the content we expected to find. But when the concept of 'nothing' is referred to God, God is clothed with a power that indicates his superiority. God is superior to nature; that is, there is something that is above it and on which it depends. But what is this 'it' nature actually? And who is really this 'he', God, creator of all that exists?

For a long time nature was believed to be the planet Earth, which pre-dated human beings and from which we were formed, first man and then woman. And it was from this earthly nature/matter given life by the divine breath that we were engendered. We too became partly creatures of nature.

We were handed over to nature to live in it and subdue it. We draw our sustenance from it and make our history in it. Living in it and from it, we discover the laws that regulate it and submit ourselves to these. This leads to some things coming to be viewed as natural, others unnatural, and others artificial. In effect, this classification ends by becoming a convention and a type of morality on the basis of which behaviours are judged as conforming to or transgressing a pre-established order. In this way, a natural order is composed, often identified with the will of God or, more precisely, the will of a concept of God. We seldom reflect on the meaning of this natural order. And when we try to think about it, we come up against the religious authority of those who uphold it and declare it to be something independent of evolution and of human understanding. This is why we can say that the basis of resistance to any cultural shift in regard to the concept of nature lies in the philosophical-religious conception identified with the will of God.

Ecclesiastical power constituted as *Magisterium* states that before this divine order we can only bow our heads and obey. The clergy and their subordinates have publicly to preach and administer this unchallengeable obedience, since it is considered to be revealed by God. This revelation seems to have nothing to do with the temporal and cultural contingencies in which we live: it is a pre-ordained order and has to command the present and its multiple developments. In this way a sort of boundary is set up between the will of God and the will of human beings, as though it were a barrier that cannot be crossed, a barrier that also sets a limit to human life and morality. This situation can be a starting point for developing a political and ethical reflection on the notion of nature and on the social power of those who administer this position. Besides this, we could reflect on the utilitarian use they make of the discoveries of science, on the model of reasoning they employ, and on their models of God and the sort of 'holy war' they have waged to defend their positions.

Today, well into the twenty-first century, we are witnessing an incredible dislocation between scientific and cultural advances in many fields of human knowledge and Christian religious culture, which often reflects medieval attitudes. This statement is not designed to turn religion into a sort of scientific discourse, but it does seek to open new horizons based on the current historical reality. In the same way that we can ask the sciences to become less elitist and to construct ways of democratizing their discoveries to benefit a wider range of people, we can ask the theologies of the Churches to re-think their philosophical concepts and to re-structure catechesis and pastoral practice on a new basis.

II. Human beings and masculine reason subduing nature

In the order of creation human beings were considered to be part of nature and at the same time distinct from it. Although they need nature to live, they can understand it and subdue it. This distinction was based on human reason being viewed as belonging to the spiritual order, linked to the spiritual soul created directly by God. The human soul does not belong to the order of nature but is a spiritual principle, the divine image and likeness. This logic of rationality naturally involves hierarchies, and so the first being elevated to the excellence of spiritual reasoning is the male. Women are only secondarily rational, even though after long discussions they were granted a spiritual soul. The logical coherence of this perception of human beings and of nature corresponded to a hierarchical view of living beings, typically classified by Aristotle – whose heirs we are – into ranks of animate and inanimate beings.

We know that in the patriarchal tradition nature outside human beings was classed as a 'place', and as a place it became an *object* subjected to men's use and power. It was the man who named beings and subdued them. This led to nature considered an object to be conquered also becoming a market place.

On this basis we can make a critical evaluation, which is now accepted by the majority of Churches, of the excesses of human power over nature and the disastrous consequences of our domination of the planet. The connection between a classist vision of society and the reduction of nature to an object can be clearly seen in struggles for agrarian reform, for just division of land, and for the need to abolish the monocultures that are damaging the soil and human life. But we need to go further. We need to see how our philosophies, our beliefs, and our theological concepts still uphold various forms of domination or present a neutral face while we continue on our path to self-destruction. There is a significant gap between ethical discourse on the dignity of the planet and the maintenance of hierarchical and excluding attitudes in daily life.

III. Woman nature

There is a sort of 'naturalist' concept of women that functions in different cultures and particularly in Christianity. There is no space here for an exhaustive discussion of how this concept arose, so I just note that that a sort of primordial feminine lives in all of us. We bear the marks of our origins, of the waters in the womb and even of the waters in which life seems to have come into being. We have something like an intuitive grasp of a primitive sacred feminine to which all beings owe their origin. It is as though this 'first mother' were the original matter or the prime nature from which we come, matter predating even the rise of so-called masculine power. This is not like the patriarchal concept of nature as a second reality, created by a God with a historically masculine face. It is rather a vital, even biological, anteriority predating the concept of God as creator. Witnesses to this primordial experience are the devotions to Mother Earth, fertility goddesses, and the many Madonnas born out of Christianity. This degree of grandeur was, for reasons that are both clear and obscure, paradoxically reduced to an object of domination and cult. It was made to seem inferior, silenced, and colonized, but it endlessly re-emerges as a source of life that cannot be ignored in the many cultures that comprise humankind.

The symbolism of our origins shows itself in many ways. It is expressed in the precariousness and ambiguity of the conjunction of nature, matter, and *mater*. The concept of nature is thereby opened up to a synthesis of material realities, a synthesis of our paradoxical experience that everything is created and re-created on the basis of the feminine. In some ways, from this viewpoint and starting from a phenomenological reading key, what we call nature is on the one hand above all forms of rationalization concerning it and on the other the condition for all of them. So we might say analogically, 'In the beginning there were the maternal waters' or 'In the beginning there was the Mother', the Material Word out of which everything was created. All was contained in the Mother, the *feminine*, in the complexity of nature. Everything was made out of this, and nothing that exists can exist without it. . . . Here, symbolism touches on the reality of our life experience.

For this reason, rather than return to the Father's house or the paternal embrace, we return to the Mother and to the bosom that has already been our source of warmth. This feminine power, previously objectivized and mercantilized, is today breaking out in several different social movements and in the new feminist philosophies and theologies that are seeing the light in various parts of the world. This is not a matter of absolutizing the Mother but rather of recovering her power and symbolism in an effort to overcome the distortions under which we currently live.

Conclusion and further thoughts

A consideration of the concept of nature starting from other reference points is not just essential for a reflection on ecology; it is an equally urgent need if we are to recover the Christian tradition in a living form. A theology founded on hierarchical philosophical concepts originating in cultural worlds now well distant from our own can no longer provide an account of today's requirements. We urgently need to re-weave our human tapestry, our brotherly and sisterly bonds, through repossessing our religious traditions and the many forms of wisdom we have created. And repossessing them means re-creating them on the basis of the challenges our own relationships and concerns impose on us. This leads me to believe that taking on board the fact that our human world is at once nature and culture means that the whole of existence is marked by the perception of the world proper to our present situation. We humans are the thought of the world, despite the limits of such a statement. Understanding this conjunction in a non-hierarchical and non-sexist way will open the gates to a lived experience of our actions. This means that there are many things in us that go beyond us, but, at the same time, there is always something that affirms our dynamic capacity for loving those fallen by the wayside, strangers, orphans, forests, and rivers. There is something in us that invites us to perceive them too as extensions of our own bodies, even as we know the limits of our individuality. Perception of our inter-dependence in relation to all that exists should help us to recognize the need to overcome the hierarchical and self-centred individualism that has taken charge of us, and to overcome this not just intellectually but through simple everyday actions capable of re-building meaning and sustaining our lives. Was it not the simplicity of breaking bread, of dividing tunics, of admiring the lilies of the field, of setting prisoners free that we took as the main guidelines for our lives? Was it not the simplicity of becoming a neighbour to others and of accepting ourselves as neighbour of others that became the major indicator of the presence of transcendence in our midst? Sharing our daily bread through public policy and closeness to the poor is the insistent road on which life itself has set us. To welcome this proclamation on the basis of new reference points is one of the great challenges of our time.

Translated by Paul Burns

Short Bibliography

Gebara, Ivone. *Intuiciones ecofeministas – ensayo para repensar el concocimiento y la religión*. Montevideo: Doble Clic, 1998.

———. *Compartir los panes y los peces – Cristianismo, teología y teología feminista*. Montevideo: Doble Clic, 2008.

Mies, Maria and Vandana Shiva. *Ecofeminism*. London & New York: Zed Books, 1993.

Ress, Judith. *Ecofeminism in Latin America*. Maryknoll, NY: Orbis Books, 2006.

Ruether, Rosemary Radford. *Gaia and God – An Ecofeminist Theology of Earth Healing*. New York: HarperCollins, 1992.

Zizek, Slavoj, Eric L. Santner, and Kenneth Reinhard. *The Neighbor: Three Inquiries in Political Theology*. Chicago: University of Chicago Press, 2006.

Opinion on Ethical Aspects of Synthetic Biology of the European Group on Ethics in Science and New Technologies (EGE) presented to the European Commission

HILLE HAKER

New developments in science have to do with our particular understanding of 'nature', with which natural law is concerned, if only indirectly. In recent years this understanding has become a matter of contention because interest in the possibility of modifying nature has focussed increasingly on the biological aspects of human nature.

Philosophy and theology start with the idea of human nature as something that can be changed, at least insofar as behaviour is concerned. There would be no ethics and ultimately no morals if nature were unalterable. By tradition, of course, theology is sure that human nature is constitutionally non-contingent. An 'inclination' to 'evil' and to 'good' is said to be just as much part of human nature as its social character, or the basic relation of a human being to others, and in the end to God, which determines the *telos* (the ultimate form of fulfilment) of human existence. The notion of the teleological nature of life dates back to Aristotle, and the concept of natural law transfers it to human nature. In this application the intellectual faculties (or a person's rational nature) above all else are seen as comprising the central dimension of a human being's inherent teleology. In its theological acceptation, the conceptual framework of this idea is extended to include the derivation of the human being (as, ultimately, of nature as a whole) from God, so that the human *telos* is not restricted to self-fulfilment, but consists in its accordance with God's redemptive action.

This traditional view interprets changes in human behaviour on the basis of human nature as it exists but in the context of God's saving activity. This entirely preserves the 'specific value' of human nature, for there can be no fundamental conflicts between the fulfilment of human nature (of its needs

130

and purposive aspects) and the divine 'plan'. Admittedly there can be 'deviations' from nature in what is taken to be the normative sense, but these deviations occur only because of erroneous interpretations, or because of a weak will and culpable behaviour. This idea of human nature has its counterpart in traditional science when nature is seen as malleable quite apart from its constitutive conditions. In contradistinction to the natural-law tradition, the 'normativity of nature' is a matter of indifference for science, which sees nature as an object of research or (and this is increasingly the case) as a starting-point for intervening in things as they are in order to modify them as human desires and needs might require.

Nowadays the natural sciences analyze the constitutive conditions of human and extra-human nature in many different respects and in increasing detail. Decyphering the human genetic code may be seen as achieving the ultimate aim of research into the 'code of life', but also as the beginning of a new possibility. This would be an approach that no longer views 'nature' as such as the factual state of things but sees it instead as a spur to carry out an infinite series of (technical) operations to transform the constitutive conditions of life itself.

One area where the different concepts of the status of nature are especially liable to collide is 'enhancement', or the pinpointed use of technological means to improve human nature. The claims of enhancement make it more radical than (even if it does not seem clearly distinct from) widely accepted forms of intervention in (human) nature, which aim either to compensate for functional deficiencies, or to help a personality to develop by, say, various forms of education and cultivation. The division of human life into 'natural' aspects on the one hand, and 'transformable' dimensions on the other hand, is unsuccessful, because it is now possible to use enhancement, that is, the means proper to biology, neurosciences, information technology, and engineering sciences, to control forms of behaviour that were traditionally subjected to systematic exercise and concentrated effort. But this would deprive the 'nature' to which the tradition of natural law referred in various ways of the descriptive and normative outlines by which it was defined.

Modern biotechnologies originated in the second half of the twentieth century. At first they investigated the laws on which individual life processes were based and sought to elucidate the multitude of forms afforded by biological life and described by traditional biology. On this basis they started an increasingly intensive examination of the ways in which biological organisms function. Currently, biotechnology – a combination of biology, information technology, physics and chemistry – is moving beyond that research.

For some decades researchers have been analyzing the genetic structures of life, altering them, and reassembling them. Until now, however, they have used 'natural' genes in these studies and have restricted themselves to their recomposition.

The shades of similarity and difference between the 'genetic manipulation' of organisms and 'synthetic biology' are rather recondite and are still a matter of controversy among scientists. Nevertheless, there is evidence to support a definition that emphasizes the use of unnatural DNA sequences or modules as a criterion for distinguishing between genetic engineering and synthetic biology.

At present researchers in the still novel research field known as 'synthetic biology 'are trying to change existing organisms by producing and synthesizing artificial genes or proteins and metabolic or developmental processes, which are intended to supplement existing biological systems with entirely new functions. In such cases, some researchers confine their efforts to modifying – and accordingly to supplementing – existing biological systems, whereas others plan to construct entirely new genes and chromosomes – and therefore quite new forms of 'life'. A possible definition of 'synthetic biology' would comprise: (1) the design of minimal cells/organisms (including a minimal genome); (2) the identification and use of biological components; and (3) the construction of biological systems that are partly or wholly artificial.

If research aims were to change, considerable areas of human life would be affected by synthetic biology – not least of all our understanding of 'nature'.

'We have got to the point in human history where we simply do not have to accept what nature has given us,'[1] says Jay Keasling, an eminent researcher trying to use synthetic biology to produce artesiminin, the source material for the leading anti-malarial drug, which has been extracted to date by a complex process from *Artemisia annua*, or sweet wormwood. Artesiminin is currently the most prominent example of how medical drugs can be developed with the aid of synthetic biology that are not only of use to industrial nations but could prove of help in combating malaria, one of the worst global infectious diseases.[2]

Accordingly, there is a twofold aim to this new direction in research: on the one hand, it seeks to obtain a better understanding of vital processes; on the other hand, however, it hopes to reconstruct biological materials, or to combine artificial DNA with natural organisms, in order to 'construct' new organisms. The range of possible applications – at least, as far as the researchers' wish-list is concerned – covers almost all those areas that are currently subject to particular social interest and concern: energy procurement, combating pollutants and toxic substances, medicine and the cosmetic industry, and agriculture as a source of foodstuffs and textiles.

Since 'synthetic biology' has already aroused similar expectations to those awakened by gene technology a few decades ago, various associations of scientists and advisory bodies have begun to investigate research in respect of its goals, means, social and economic expectations, but also its risks and its more inclusive consequences. The most comprehensive opinion of this kind was prepared by the advisory group on ethics associated with the European Commission; this appeared at the end of 2009.

The European Group on Ethics in Science and New Technologies (EGE)[3] produces Opinions for the European Commission based on studies of new developments in science and the new technologies. Its role is advisory. It can exert an (indirect) influence on the promotion of research, on legal regulation by the European Commission, but also on the political strategies developed by the European Commission. EGE Opinions are produced on the initiative of a specific Chair of the Commission and by a group of about fifteen people representing different disciplines and as far as possible reflecting the different contexts united in the European Union. Nevertheless, members do not represent any national or other interests but subscribe to a declaration regarding their scientific independence. Opinions are intended to prepare or accompany political regulation by the European Commission. This regulation is supported by the European Parliament, but the Parliament cannot introduce any bills unilaterally.

In recent years, by way of two fundamental legal documents – the Lisbon Treaty and the Charter of Fundamental Rights of the European Union – the European Commission has confirmed certain fundamental ethical rights and values and has provided a basis for determining, say, the ethical criteria required to assess fields of research.[4]

Synthetic biology, like any other technology, must be subject to the internationally approved framework of ethics and human rights. This applies especially to heeding the requirements of human dignity, which has been conceived not only as a fundamental right but as the basis of fundamental rights. Other ethical principles that also have to be observed include security, sustainability, justice, precautions for the future, freedom of research, and proportionality.

The EGE's Opinion on synthetic biology of 18 November 2009 mentions the possible areas of application that require ethical evaluation: the production and development of biofuels, the production of textiles and cosmetics, the development of diagnostic and therapeutic devices, and the development of vaccines and medicines, nutritional and animal-feed supplements, and anti-pollutant procedures.

Yet the evaluation of synthetic biology has to do not only with these areas of application, but equally with the ways in which 'life' and 'nature' are defined. A reductionist approach is questionable when, for instance, it tends emphatically to play down epigenetic influences on the development of organisms compared with the role of synthetic DNA – which could however prove to be an error with far-reaching consequences. But, from a philosophical viewpoint, it is also necessary to challenge another form of reductionism: namely, a definition of 'life' and 'nature' (in the sense of biological life processes) that does not identify the ethical aspects of these concepts and thus make their values conspicuous, even though this is an essential element of ethical interpretation, alongside other forms of analysis.

Synthetic biology would seem to evade or render obsolete the distinction between nature and artifice. But what does this imply for the evaluation of human nature and, even more importantly, what does it mean for the concept of human dignity, which philosophers think of traditionally as intimately associated with the nature of reason and self-determination? What does it mean to talk of 'artificial life' or 'living machines'? Does this call in question our image of humanity, which acts as a yardstick not only for traditional natural law but for the modern tradition of human rights?

In the ethical section of its opinion on synthetic biology, the EGE refers in particular to biosafety, both to the process itself and to certain aspects more often comprised under biosecurity, in the sense of protection against danger or threats from military but also from terrorist applications, or from the production of new biological weapons.

The EGE Opinion also contains a number of practical recommendations for the European Commission.[5]

1. *Biological safety*

The EGE advocates approving the use of products emanating from synthetic biology only on condition that specific safety prescriptions, which the Opinion identifies as requiring revision, are observed. The EGE recommends that desirable measures to be taken by the EU Commission should include the initiation of an inquiry into risk-assessment procedures in the EU, with results that could serve as a basis for repairing possible deficiencies in existing bio-safety regulations. The EGE also states that it is imperative to prepare a code of conduct governing research in the field of synthetic biology.

2. Environmental applications

The EGE also recommends that a long-term ecological impact assessment should be carried out before an organism produced or modified by synthetic biology is released into the environment. The results of this study should be evaluated with reference to the precautionary principle and measures provided for in EU legislation (the Directive on the deliberate release into the environment of genetically modified organisms).

3. Energy and renewable processes in the chemical industry

The EGE advocates that the use of synthetic biology for alternative supplies in member States should be implemented so as to complement the EU renewable energy plan. The EGE believes that the protection of consumer rights must be of primary importance. Therefore it insists on assessing the possibility of identifiable labelling of specific products resulting from synthetic biology, such as cosmetics and textiles.

4. Biomedical and biopharmaceutical applications

In cases in which synthetic-biology protocols give rise to medical drugs and medicinal products, the EGE recommends that responsible authorities such as the European Medicines Agency (EMA) should not only apply the conditions proper to scientific and legal frameworks but address specific ethical considerations.

5. Biosecurity, prevention of bioterrorism, and dual uses

Novel materials such as biomaterials or bioweapons for military use can be produced with the aid of synthetic biology. When analyzing ethical aspects of the case, the aim of security has to be weighed against that of transparency. The EGE also recommends the introduction of control mechanisms such as the issue of licences and the registration of the tools used by synthetic biology, in order to prevent the use of synthetic biology for terrorist purposes. The group also recommends that the Convention on the Prohibition of the Development, Production and Stockpiling of Bacteriological (biological) Weapons and Toxin Weapons and that their destruction should incorporate provisions on the limitation or prohibition of research activities in the field of synthetic biology.

6. Governance

In all probability the existing legislative framework of EU member States, which lacks uniformity, will prove to be inadequate. Therefore the EGE emphatically urges the Commission to propose, and to put in place in the EU, a robust governance framework for synthetic biology, in which the relevant stakeholders and their specific areas of responsibility are named. The EGE proposes that the EU should raise the theme of the governance of synthetic biology in relevant global fora.

7. Patents and a common heritage

The EGE recommends the initiation of debates on the most appropriate way to ensure public access to the results of synthetic biology. The group stresses the importance of ensuring that ethical questions of general relevance that arise in connection with patent applications should be duly raised within the framework of the system for granting patents. According to the EU Patent Directive, the EGE is the body responsible for assessing the ethical aspects of specific patents. The EGE emphatically urges the European Patent Office and the national Patent Offices to take account of, and implement, Article 7 of European Patent Directive 98/44.

8. Trade and world law

The ethical aspects of synthetic biology should be addressed in discussions of this technology at an international level, including the World Trade Organization (WTO). This point should also be taken into account in the context of the Doha Round negotiations. The EGE emphatically calls on the EU to set norms for the biological safety of products resulting from synthetic biology as minimum standards for the introduction of such products into the EU and for their export from the EU.

9. Dialogue between science and society

The group calls on the EU and its member States to implement measures to promote public debate and the commitment of the different players, in order to discover which areas of application of synthetic biology arouse the greatest degree of concern in society.

10. Research

The group calls on the Commission to support the basic research and applied and interdisciplinary research in the areas of biology, chemistry, energy, and materials science and engineering described in the Opinion, and to propose appropriate means to reflect this in the budget for the EU Research Framework Programmes. The group also notes that synthetic biology could lead to a paradigm shift in the future with regard to understanding concepts of life. Therefore it calls on the Commission to initiate an open intercultural forum to examine the abovementioned topics, including philosophical and religious questions.

Translated by J. G. Cumming

Notes

1. 'A Life of Its Own', *The New Yorker*, 28 Sept. 2009.
2. Here it is not a matter of debating the extent of any possible existing resistance to artesiminin and then of necessarily re-assessing research efforts. We are concerned with research perspectives and not to evaluate the specific contents of particular instances of research.
3. For all opinions as well as information on the composition and activities of the group, see http://ec.europa.eu/european_group_ethics/index_en.htm
4. In other words, the assessment of technologies is based on a normative-ethical framework which certainly has to be ethically grounded (in the context, say, of an ethics of human rights), but one which, as far as the European Union is concerned, member States have already recognized as binding. The Lisbon Treaty should not be thought of as a constitution. It is a treaty.
5. With regard to the following pages, see the original press release at http://ec.europa.eu/european_group_ethics/docs/press_release_opinion_25_de.pdf; for the whole Opinion see http://ec.europa.eu/european_group_ethics/docs/opinion25_en.pdf; for further opinions, consult http://ec.europa.eu/european_group_ethics/avis/index_en.htm.

Contributors

MARÍA CHRISTINA A. ASTORGA is the Founding Director of the Center for the Study of Catholic Social Thought at Duquesne University. She was the former Chair of the Theology Department of the Ateneo de Manila University-Loyola Schools and was a professor of moral theology at the Loyola School of Theology in the Philippines. She was a visiting scholar at Weston Jesuit School of Theology; a Fellow at the Jesuit Institute of Boston College and Woodstock Theological Center at Georgetown University; and a visiting professor at the University of San Diego and Canisius College.

Address: 112 Washington Place, 12 G, Pittsburgh, PA 15219, USA

JACQUINEAU AZÉTSOP is originally from Cameroon and holds a PhD in theology from Boston College (USA) and a Master's in Public Health from Johns Hopkins University (USA). He is lecturer in health policy and bioethics at the Faculté de Médécine Teilhard de Chardin in N'djaména, Chad; and visiting lecturer in bioethics and public health at N'djaména University School of Medicine. His research focuses on African culture, theology and philosophy and bioethics; social epidemiology and bioethics; and the link between politics, ethics and public health on issues such as road traffic safety, obesity, food security, and health education. He has published in *Developing World Bioethics, Philosophy, Ethics and Humanities in Medicine*, and *Journal of Public Health Ethics*.

Address: Communaute Paul Miki, B.P. 456 N'djamena, Chad (Central Africa)

IVONE GEBARA is a Brazilian Sister of Our Lady (Canonesses of St Augustine) and one of Latin America's leading theologians, writing from the perspective of ecofeminism and liberation theology. She is a professor at the Theological Institute of Recife. Among her works are *Longing for Running*

Water: Ecofeminism and Liberation, and *Out of the Depths: Women's Experience of Evil and Salvation*.

Address: Rua Luis Jorge Dos Santos, 278 Tabatinga, Camaragibe PE, 54756-380 Camaragibe PE, Brazil
E-mail: ivone@hotlink.com.br

HILLE HAKER is Professor of Moral Theology and Social Ethics, Goethe University/Frankfurt, and Chair for Catholic Moral Theology, Loyola University Chicago. She has written books on moral identity and narrative ethics, and a social ethics approach to human reproduction and genetic diagnosis at the beginning of human life. She has edited several books, is a member of the European Group on Science and New Technologies of the European Commission and a member of the Board of Editors of *Concilium*.

Address: Goethe-Universität Frankfurt, FB Kath. Theologie – Ethik, Grüneburgplatz 1, 60629 Frankfurt am Main, Germany
E-mail: h.haker@em.uni-frankfurt.de or hhaker@luc.edu.

KENNETH R. HIMES is a Franciscan friar, born in Brooklyn, NY, in 1950. For many years he taught at the Washington (DC) Theological Union and for the past six years he has been associate professor and chairman in the theology department at Boston College. He received his Ph.D. in religion and public policy from Duke University. His areas of research include Catholic social teaching, ethical issues in war and peace, and American Catholic social reform movements.

Address: Department of Theology, Boston College, 140 Commonwealth Avenue, Chestnut Hill, MA 02467, USA

STEPHEN J. POPE received his Ph.D. from the University of Chicago, and is Professor of Theological Ethics at Boston College. He is the author of *The Evolution of Altruism and the Ordering of Love* (1994) and *Human Evolution and Christian Ethics* (2007). Current areas of research include virtue ethics and the ethics of peace, war, reconciliation, justice, and social reconstruction.

Address: 21 Campanella Way, Room 319, Boston College, Chestnut Hill, MA 02467, USA

EBERHARD SCHOCKENHOFF teaches moral theology at the Albert-Ludwigs-Universität in Freiburg. He is Editor-in-Chief of the *Zeitschrift für Medzinische Ethik* and a member of the German Council for Ethics. He has published several works on the foundations of ethics and specific problems in medical ethics. His latest published work is *Ethik des Lebens. Grundlagen und neue Herausforderungen* (2009).

Address: Albert-Ludwigs-Universität Freiburg, Institut für Systematische Theologie AB Moraltheologie, Platz der Universität, D-79085 Freiburg, Germany

LUDWIG SIEP was born in 1942 and since 1986 has been Professor of Philosophy at the University of Münster and Head of the Regional Centre for Bioethics. He is a member of the North-Rhineland–Westphalia and a corresponding member of the Bavarian Academies of Sciences as well as Chairman of the Central Ethical Commission for Embryonic Stem Cell Research. His latest publications are *Der Weg der Phänomenologie des Geistes* ([2]2001); *Konkrete Ethik* (2004); *John Locke, Zweite Abhandlung über die Regierung, Kommentar von Ludwig Siep* (2007).

Address: Philosophisches Seminar, Westfälische Wilhelms-Universität Münster, Domplatz 23, 48143 Münster, Germany

ANDRÉS TORRES QUEIRUGA was born in 1940 and is Professor of Philosophy of Religion and Fundamental Theology at the University of Santiago de Compostela. His main interest is working for an understandable and livable faith in (post)modern culture. His two key concerns are: (1) to rethink the concept of revelation while keeping strictly to the idea of 'the God who creates out of love', applying it to principal theological topics; and (2) to insist on the commitment to an 'evangelical (super)democratic' renewal of ecclesial government. He is editor of *Encrucillada: Revista Galega de Pensamento Cristián*, as well as being on the editorial board of *Iglesia Viva*, an advisor to *Revista Portuguesa de Filosofia*, and a member of the Board of Editors of *Concilium*. His many published works include *Constitución y evolución del dogma* (1977); *Recuperar la salvación* (1977, [3]2001); *Creo en Dios Padre* ([5]1998); *Recuperar la creación* (1997; German trans. 2008); *Fin del cristianismo premoderno* (2000); *Repensar la resurrección* (2003); *Esperanza a pesar del mal*

(2005); *Repensar la revelación* (2008; revised ed. of 1977, trans. into Italian, Portuguese and German).

Address: Facultade de Filosofía, 15782 Santiago, Spain
E-mail: atorres@usc.es/torresqueiruga@gmail.com

CRISTINA L. H. TRAINA is Associate Professor of Religious Studies at Northwestern University in Evanston, Illinois, USA. Her interests include the just treatment and moral agency of children; ethics of sexuality; migration; and questions of natural law and feminist method. Her published works include *Feminist Ethics and Natural Law: The End of the Anathemas* (1998).

Address: Department of Religious Studies, Northwestern University, Crowe Hall 5-179, 1860 Campus Drive, Evanston, IL 60208-2164, USA

ANDREA VICINI, MD, PhD, is a Jesuit priest and Associate Professor of Moral Theology and Bioethics at the Faculty of Theology of Southern Italy at S. Luigi in Naples and, currently, Gasson Chair Professor at Boston College. His areas of research include reproductive technologies, end of life issues, genetics, and biotechnologies. Among his publications is *Genetica umana e bene comune* (2008).

Address: 246 Beacon Street, Chestnut Hill, MA 02467, USA

JEAN-PIERRE WILS was born in Geel in Belgium in 1957. He studied philosophy and Catholic theology at Louvain and Tübingen. He holds a chair at the Radboud University of Nijmegen in the Netherlands, teaches the cultural theory of morals with special reference to religion, and is Dean of the religious studies faculty. He has written widely on ethics and on current ethical and religio-political conflicts.

Address: Stiftsgasse 1, D 47559 Kranenburg, Germany

Concilium Subscription Information

February   2010/1: *Ministries in the Church*

April   2010/2: *The Bible as Word of God*

June   2010/3: *Human Nature, Human Goods, and Natural Law*

October   2010/4: *Atheists of What God?*

December   2010/5: *Indigenous Theologies*

New subscribers: to receive *Concilium 2010* (five issues) anywhere in the world, please copy this form, complete it in block capitals and send it with your payment to the address below.

- -

Please enter my subscription for *Concilium 2010*

Individuals
____ £40.00 UK
____ £60.00 overseas
____ $110.00 North America/Rest of World
____ €99.00 Europe

Institutions
____ £55.00 UK
____ £75.00 overseas
____ $140 North America/Rest of World
____ €125.00 Europe

Postage included – airmail for overseas subscribers

Payment Details:

Payment must accompany all orders and can be made by cheque or credit card
I enclose a cheque for £/$/€ _____ Payable to Hymns Ancient and Modern
Please charge my Visa/MasterCard (Delete as appropriate) for £/$/€ _____
Credit card number ---
Expiry date ---
Signature of cardholder --
Name on card --
Telephone --------------------E-mail --------------------------------------

Send your order to *Concilium*, Hymns Ancient and Modern
13–17 Long Lane, London EC1A 9PN, UK
E-Mail: office@hymnsam.co.uk

Customer service information:
All orders must be prepaid. Subscriptions are entered on an annual basis (i.e. January to December). No refunds on subscriptions will be made after the first issue of the Journal has been despatched. If you have any queries or require information about other payment methods, please contact our Customer Services department.